INSIDE
SONGWRITING

GETTING TO THE HEART OF CREATIVITY

Jason Blume

Billboard Books
An imprint of Watson-Guptill Publications
New York

Senior Acquisitions Editor: Bob Nirkind
Project Editor: Meryl Greenblatt
Interior design by : Michelle Gengaro-Kokmen
Cover design by: Cooley Design Lab
Production Manager: Ellen Greene

First published in 2003 by
Watson-Guptill Publications,
a division of VNU Business Media, Inc.,
770 Broadway, New York, NY 10003
www.watsonguptill.com

Library of Congress Cataloging-in-Publication Data
for this title may be obtained from the Library of Congress
Library of Congress Card Number: 2002115276
ISBN: 0-8230-8361-6

Printed in the United States

First printing, 2003

1 2 3 4 5 6 7 8 9 / 10 09 08 07 06 05 04 03

INSIDE
SONGWRITING

GETTING TO THE HEART OF CREATIVITY

ACKNOWLEDGMENTS

I could never have written this book without the assistance and support of Neil Rice. Neil—you really are amazing. A heartfelt "thank you" to my editor Bob Nirkind, my wonderful literary agent, Rita Rosenkranz, and project editor, Meryl Greenblatt.

I'd like to acknowledge my appreciation to Mark Mason, Deanna Bruton, Gabrielle Hoffman, Julie Jarett, and the staff at BMI, as well as Bart Herbison and the staff at NSAI, and Michael Laskow, Michael Lederer, Doug Minnick, and the staff at Taxi for helping me to bring my lessons to so many songwriters. I'd also like to thank all of those who work so hard to help me find homes for my songs: Amy Smith-Heinz, David Gray, Eric Beall, Lynn Gann, Adam Ryan, Pat Finch, Janet Barnes, and Clint Newcom at Zomba. Rachelle Greenblatt and Kevin Lamb went above and beyond in helping me secure permissions to reprint lyrics. Thank you so much.

Last but not least, I'd like to thank Maris and Mark Goldberg, Karen Taylor-Good, Claire Ulanoff, Maureen Custer, Janice Cook, Virginia Rice, Ilene Krems, Wayne Moore, Bryan and Holly Cumming, Carol Elliott, Buddy Mondlock, Kathy Johnson, Leslie Brenner, the Werlin Clan, Gary Baker, Jane Snyder, Jamie and Adam Goldberg, Todd and Laura Serinsky, Katy Garvey, and Barbara Rothstein for their powerful love and support.

DEDICATION

This book is dedicated with much gratitude to Michael Hollandsworth, who believed in my talent and used tough love to teach me how to be the best songwriter I could be.

It's also dedicated to the memory of my father, Ned Blume, who encouraged me to make up stories to go with the music he played for me. I know he's playing his mandolin every night in heaven and giving pennies to the angels who can "name that tune."

TABLE OF CONTENTS

INTRODUCTION

I spent more than eleven years dreaming of becoming a successful songwriter and doing everything in my power to make that dream come true. During much of that time it felt as though the success I wanted so desperately was impossible to attain—as though I were separated from my goal by an invisible, impenetrable wall.

It felt as if those lucky people who wrote the hits must have had magic dust sprinkled on them, while I was waiting in the wrong line. But I was mistaken. There were tools and techniques that I needed to master before I'd be able to write the kind of songs that would earn me the acclaim I so very much wanted.

You might say my journey officially began in August 1979, when I announced to my family and friends that I had resigned from my job as a psychiatric aide in a Philadelphia hospital and was moving to Los Angeles to become a famous singer and songwriter. I loaded all of my possessions that could be crammed into my little Datsun Honeybee. If it didn't fit, it got left behind.

I had a total of $400 to pay for the food and gas it would take to get me cross-country; and this was long before I acquired a collection of credit cards. Since I didn't have enough money for hotels, I bought a little one-man pup tent that would become my home, either in a campground or park, each night after a long day's drive. To save money on restaurants, I brought along a cooler filled with food—summer sausage, yogurt, dried fruit, and scrambled eggs that I'd frozen. I didn't know where I would stay when I reached California, but I was young and much too excited to be as worried as I probably should have been.

I remember pulling away as my family and closest friends waved goodbye. On some level I think I knew I'd never live close by again. I've never been someone who cries easily, but I sobbed uncontrollably for almost an hour as I watched life as I'd known it disappear in my rearview mirror.

After twelve hours of driving, I pulled off the road that first night at a campground in Ohio. Surrounded by huge RVs, I was the only camper in a tent. Before drifting off to sleep, I used my flashlight to read a book about "making it" in the music business. Someone had given it to me as a going-away present.

Around 5:00 a.m., I woke up drenched, lying in several inches of water. It was pouring and I hadn't spent the extra money to buy a waterproof tent. I decided to thaw out my scrambled eggs over a can of Sterno before hitting the road. When I opened my cooler, it appeared to be alive, overflowing with maggots. The cooler went into the dumpster and I hit the interstate. This trip was not getting off to a good start.

Except for a brief encounter with a snake, the remaining twenty-four hundred miles were relatively uneventful, until I crossed the Rocky Mountains. Stretched across the Colorado sky, I saw something I had never seen before—a spectacular double rainbow. I took it as a sign, an omen that I was on the right path and that my dreams were waiting to come to life with all the beauty of that rainbow.

I was certain that I'd be an overnight success, with a house in Beverly Hills and a Mercedes in the driveway within the first year. That's not the way my life unfolded. I struggled for more than eleven years before I could proudly say that although I only earned a meager living, I earned it as a professional songwriter.

Today, my songs are on albums that have sold more than forty-five million copies, and I've worked with some of the biggest names in the music industry. Several of my songs have been included on Grammy-nominated albums. I've received awards and honors and have seen my songs on Billboard's Pop, Country, and R&B charts—*all at the same time*. I guess my dream to become a successful songwriter has indeed come true! The stories that comprise this book provide insight into how I made it happen.

I've learned some powerful lessons about songwriting as well as life along the way, and my education continues to this day. For example, while there are no "rules" in songwriting, I now understand that there are tools and techniques that can help us write better material. I've learned that even when it's not easy, I can identify those skills I need to strengthen, and improve upon them with practice. I've learned that I can survive devastating disappointment and that I chose a career that can be frustrating, stressful, maddening—and incredible. Perhaps the most important thing I've learned is that with hard work, perseverance, and, of course, some luck, we can accomplish things that seem impossible.

I've also found that my greatest passion in life is teaching. Some of my most gratifying moments have been spent teaching my songwriting techniques and encouraging aspiring writers throughout the U.S. and beyond to follow their dreams. I've had an opportunity to share what I've learned with thousands of writers who read my book, *6 Steps to Songwriting Success: The Comprehensive Guide to Writing and Marketing Hit Songs* (Billboard Books), and with those who attended my workshops.

I'd like to thank each person who took the time to write and tell me the ways that my book impacted his or her life. Those letters and e-mails mean a great deal to me. By sharing the lessons I've learned along my journey, I hope I can help you with yours.

THE BLANK PAGE

I'm staring at a blank page right now and wondering what to write about. "Well," it occurs to me, "how about writing about fear of the blank page?" Throughout the years, in order to avoid beginning work on a song, I've scrubbed, vacuumed, and polished surfaces that had never before had even a passing acquaintance with Mr. Clean. Other writers I've spoken with have confessed to similar experiences. I suspect we've suffered from the dreaded *blankpageaphobia*. Untreated, chronic cases can sometimes develop into full-blown writer's block.

"So, what makes you think you could ever be successful?" "The odds are one in a million." "How long are you going to give this nonsense until you get a real job?" I heard those comments at least a thousand times. Sometimes they came from my father. More often they came from the little voice inside my head. *Gosh, I can't imagine why it would be frightening to begin.*

My guess is that, for most of us, the basis of this fear is finding out that we're not good enough; that we're untalented, unworthy frauds. That being the case, let's think about what "good enough" means. How is "good enough" measured in a creative endeavor? I've always been very results oriented. For eleven-and-a-half years I worked day jobs that I loathed, all the while dreaming of becoming a famous songwriter. During those lean years, was I a "failure" each time I wrote a song that didn't get recorded? It often felt that way.

Every time I had a song critiqued by a professional, I secretly hoped and expected that this would be the one that would change my life. When I took classes, I wasn't there to learn which areas I needed to concentrate on and which skills I needed to practice. I was there to be "discovered," to become an overnight sensation. I wanted the goodies—the hit records, the Mercedes, the fame and fortune. I wanted to show the kids who'd made fun of me in high school how far I'd come.

When I attended workshops and had my songs evaluated, it was devastating to hear comments like, "The melody needs to be hookier," or "There are no fresh images in the lyrics," or, what I heard most often, "It just doesn't feel like a hit." My attitude became, "I'll show you how successful I can be. I'll go write a song that's so incredible, you won't be able to turn it down!"

I won't say I wasn't initially disappointed each time the prospect of a publishing deal failed to materialize. Of course I was, but looking back it's clear that I channeled that frustration into the energy and motivation to write better songs. I suspect that having something to prove to those high school bullies who still lived inside my head was probably a significant part of why I eventually became successful. That hunger and the drive to make it were good things. They were cruel, unrelenting taskmasters that didn't contribute much fun to the journey, but they kept me focused on my goal and working hard.

So, what about that blank page I mentioned at the beginning of this chapter? Look—I've already filled mine! I've probably faced thousands of such pages. Just like the one I started with today, they somehow get filled up.

With 20/20 hindsight, I see that many of those pages held songs that weren't very strong. They didn't quite deliver the message from my heart to the world in a manner that was likely to touch millions of listeners. Some of those songs were too personal for others to relate to. Others contained lyrics that weren't quite special enough. Several fell short in the melody department. The cold, hard truth is that by virtue of the definition of "best," every song we write can't be our best—and, in this business, "good" isn't good enough. The professional competition, even with a headache, can easily crank out a "good," perfectly crafted song on a bad day.

After more than twenty years of studying the tools and techniques that contribute to successful songs, on a rare occasion the stars line up in perfect harmony and one of my songs comes out just right. In those instances, a truly fresh idea flows through me as if I were a channel and I find a new, unique way of expressing myself melodically and lyrically. Unfortunately, there's no way to predict when one of those is about to pop out. So, I have to write all of those others to get to the one that's waiting at the back of the line.

I've heard it said that developing writers need to throw out the first one hundred songs they write, that those are for practice. I find that's usually the case for at least the first fifty. But looking back, it's clear that even my "bad" songs served an important purpose. I learned something from all of them, and each one was a milestone along the journey to mastering my craft.

When it comes down to it, why be afraid of that blank page? The worst thing that can happen is that I'll write a less-than-incredible song. So what? Hopefully, I'll learn something from that song that will bring me one step closer to writing one of those "Wow" songs.

Exercise

What do you *really* want to write about? For now, forget about trying to be "commercial" and jot down three topics you'd really love to express as a song. No one ever has to see what you've written unless you choose to share it.

Now set a timer for twenty minutes and begin a song based on one of those topics. Let it come straight from your heart. Don't worry about whether it's good or not. Tell your internal critic to take the next twenty minutes off. You can rewrite and tweak later. For the purposes of this exercise, whatever you write is perfect—*as long as it expresses what you feel.* Knowing that this exercise has a deadline and that your work doesn't have to be your "best" can help take away the fear.

Some of my strongest songs and ideas were born from this exercise.

BETTER THAN THE CRAP
ON THE RADIO

There's one question I can count on being asked at virtually every seminar I teach: "Why is there so much crap on the radio?" There are several ways I address this. One is to paraphrase a well-known quote and point out, "Crap is in the ear of the beholder." What constitutes "good" or "bad" music (or, for that matter, *any* creative work) is purely subjective. That's why Baskin Robbins makes 32+ different flavors. Some people love Mocha Fudge Ripple. Others think it's horrible and prefer French Vanilla.

Some of the "crap" on the radio may not be to your personal taste, but those professionals who make the decisions thought these songs were good or they wouldn't have gotten recorded. No matter how much you saturate the airwaves with a song, millions of people won't part with their hard-earned money to buy it unless they like it.

That said, there are lots of reasons why a song might get recorded—and some of these reasons are not exclusively based on the quality of the song itself. It's true that there are sometimes political and personal reasons why a song might be chosen. Perhaps it was written by the artist's girlfriend or record producer—or by the A&R (Artists and Repertoires) person, the individual at the record label in charge of selecting songs for the project. Or maybe the artist has no taste, loved the song, and had enough clout to include it on his or her album. Complaining about these things is not a productive use of your time. Instead, try asking, "How can I get *my* songs on the radio?"

I wrote my first song when I was twelve years old. I strummed the three chords I'd learned on my father's mandolin, sang whatever came to mind, and out popped, "Eternal August." It was a terrible song by professional industry standards. The uninspired melody followed the predictable chord changes. It didn't conform to any of the structures that are typically heard on the radio—I wasn't aware that there were any structures that songs typically fit into. The stream-of-consciousness lyric I'd written was vague, self-indulgent, and devoid of any fresh, original images. And those were my song's "good" qualities.

When I sang my early songs, I thought they were terrific. My friends and family told me they were beautiful and they asked me to play them at parties. (Well, maybe they didn't exactly ask, but I'd always bring my mandolin and sing at gatherings.) I *knew* my songs were better than most of those on the radio.

Let's examine this statement: "My songs are better than most of the songs on the radio." If my songs are "better" than the songs on the radio, a logical conclusion is that there is a substantial difference between my songs and those that rise to the top of the charts and cause millions of listeners to rush out and buy various artists' CDs.

Back in my early writing days, I would light incense, sip wine, smoke pot, strum my mandolin, and unload the angst of my soul into the ether. (Except for occasionally playing the mandolin, I no longer do any of those things.) Writing was a catharsis, a means of self-expression. It was all about me. It was creativity in its purest form, and the process felt wonderful. At the time, of course, I wanted my songs to become famous and generate lots of money. I wanted to be respected and admired as a songwriter and I wanted that Mercedes in my driveway. But that's not why I wrote songs. They were deep, profound, personal expressions, and my reward came from the writing process itself—not from royalty checks.

So there I was, writing these passionate, heartfelt songs that I felt were far superior to the commercial fluff on the radio. The hit songs that comprised the Top 40 seemed completely devoid of anything resembling genuine feeling, yet they were getting lots of airplay and making their writers and performers rich and successful. I was so poor I would search for pennies behind the sofa cushions before going to the market. What was wrong with this picture?

In looking back over the journey that took me from living in one roach-infested room (no kitchen and a bathroom down the hall that I shared with the junkies, prostitutes, and hustlers who lived in the building) to earning respect and a good living as a songwriter, one thing stands out: The shift that steered me toward success began the moment I realized that indeed I was writing songs that were fundamentally different from those that were on the radio. The critical issue wasn't whether my songs were "better" or "worse." It's that there were certain elements that appeared in the vast majority of radio hits—*and that my songs did not include enough of these common denominators.*

My melodies were not consciously crafted to encourage listeners to sing along; they were whatever happened to pop out at the time. Plus, my lyrics were more personal, poetic, and symbolic than the hits on the radio. I wasn't attempting to craft my songs in a way that would connect to millions of listeners—yet that was my hope. My songs came straight from my heart, but, unfortunately, that's where they stayed.

I was moved by the melodies I wrote and understood what my lyrics intended, so I assumed that listeners would connect to my songs, too. Wrong! Songwriting is an art of communication. It may sound harsh, but listeners don't particularly care what you felt when you wrote your song if they don't feel it when they listen. For many songwriters, crafting songs that effectively communicate their feelings is a very different process from writing solely for their own satisfaction.

The songs that artists write for themselves are often quite different from the kinds of songs we can pitch to artists who do not write their own material. Why is that? Because performing songwriters are selling not just a song, but also a musical style, sound, and image. Writers who perform their own material have the latitude to write songs with lyrics that are more personal, poetic, and symbolic and less literal than those typically found in the kinds of songs that mainstream pop and country artists most often record. Singer/songwriters' melodies are sometimes quirkier, less predictable, and less repetitive than those that might be recorded by artists who don't write their own material.

If I'd had a voice as distinctive and appealing as Macy Gray, Sting, Alanis Morissette, Bono, or some of those other wonderful singers who write their own material, I would have had an ideal outlet for my songs. But I didn't. If I'd looked as good as Kylie Minogue or danced like Usher, I might have been able to succeed recording my own songs. But, alas, I didn't.

If the songs you love to write do not have an outlet in the current commercial market, does that mean you shouldn't write them? No, but confusing these songs with those that are geared to the commercial market is a recipe for frustration. If your goal is to hear your songs on the radio, you're missing your target if you're writing material that is "better" than those radio songs that *are successful*.

No one is twisting your arm, forcing you to change your style of writing. Write what you love and what moves you. However, if what you write does not fit into a current commercial format, or is not the kind of song that artists who don't write their songs record, you can either change your writing style—or simply enjoy writing as a wonderful hobby.

Exercise

Pick up a copy of *Billboard* magazine and keep it handy while you spend a couple of hours listening to those radio stations that play current hits in the style that you write (or hope to write). For example, if you write alternative rock, folk, and country songs, tune in to the different stations that play these styles.

Make a list of those songs that seem similar to the type of songs you're writing; those that have lyrical, structural, and melodic approaches that are reminiscent of your own songs. Jot down the title of each song, as well as the artist who recorded it.

Now find each of these songs on the *Billboard* chart and note who wrote and produced them. You will quickly learn whether the type of songs you are writing are being recorded by artists who do not perform their own material exclusively.

WHY WRITE SONGS?

I'm teaching at Camp SummerSongs* in New York's Catskill Mountains. In each little corner, under every tree, there seems to be someone strumming a guitar, singing, and having a wonderful time. Outside of this place, these folks are teachers, lawyers, therapists, homemakers, nurses, advertising executives, and everything in between. But for one week a year they trade their business suits for Birkenstocks and their briefcases for guitars. For seven days they leave their world behind and do what they love—singing and writing songs, surrounded by others who share their passion.

At night in coffeehouses and song circles that last until the wee hours, both the great and not-so-great songs are strutted out by their proud parents. Some of the campers sing like angels. Others . . . well, let's just say they don't. But they are having such a wonderful time that they make up in enthusiasm what they lack in pitch. They love performing and sharing a special part of who they are.

At breakfast one morning, a woman confided to me that her husband of thirty-eight years is not, and has never been, supportive of her music. She described a controlling, abusive spouse who demanded that everything go his own way. She felt that her feelings and opinions weren't important considerations to him and that she'd spent most of her life acquiescing to his demands. He told her she had no talent and would never earn any money at this, so why bother? She defended her passion like a mama lion defending her cubs and told him that she wasn't doing this for money, but for love, and that he couldn't make her stop.

She explained to me that when she wrote songs she could throw them away if she didn't like them, or she could rewrite them until she loved them. It was her choice. But in either case, the writing process itself gave her joy and she wouldn't let anyone take that away from her. She said, "Songwriting is my wings," and I believe her.

If a painting is never chosen to be displayed in a museum or a gallery, does that

*For information about Camp SummerSongs visit **www.summersongs.com**

8

mean it has no value? If a song never gets published, recorded, or played on the radio, does that mean it's worthless? Of course not. If you love creating and it makes you happy, do it. Share the beauty and joy that it brings you with those who appreciate it. If others don't like it, well, that's their loss.

ATTACH A NOTE

In October 1979 I began an eight-week workshop sponsored by ASCAP (the American Society of Composers, Authors, and Publishers). The workshop was taught by two kind and caring writers, Arthur Hamilton ("Cry Me a River") and Annette Tucker ("I Had Too Much to Dream Last Night"), in Annette's Beverly Hills home.

In that workshop, I acquired all the tools I needed to set me on the path to becoming a songwriter. My songs were placed under a proverbial microscope and critiqued each week. I learned about successful song structures, where to place titles, effective lyric writing, rhymes, the fundamentals of melodies, rewriting, and so much more.

Prior to this experience, I didn't know that the vast majority of popular songs were written employing structures or rhyme schemes. I had no idea that the title was supposed to appear in the chorus—or even that it should be anywhere within a song at all. I was like a sponge soaking up the ocean of knowledge that was offered.

Perhaps the most important things I received in those classes were encouragement and the belief that my dreams could come true. It was only a twenty-minute drive to Beverly Hills, but, when I walked through the door of Annette's lovely home, it felt as though the tiny room I rented in Hollywood was a million miles away.

I grew up in a family that was at the very bottom of the middle class and I had never been in a more beautiful house. Each Tuesday night that I attended the workshop I was exposed to more than the nuts and bolts of song crafting. I felt as though I was getting a glimpse of what life would be like someday when I became a rich and successful songwriter.

It's funny how certain things stick in our minds, and I've never forgotten a valuable lesson I learned while having a song of mine critiqued during one of those classes. In response to someone saying that she didn't understand what a portion of my lyric meant, I began explaining. But Arthur abruptly stopped me. He suggested that instead of telling the class what my lyric meant that I get a piece of paper and write out the explanation that I was about to offer. He said the next step would be to write out that clarification one million more times, *so that it could be attached to each record that would be sold.*

Of course he wasn't being literal. It was his way of teaching me that, as a songwriter, I wouldn't get the opportunity to explain my work once my song was released to the public. My job was to make my meaning clear when I wrote the song, so that my listeners would understand the story I was telling and feel the emotions I hoped my song would evoke—without any additional assistance.

That's our job all the way through the songwriting and demo process. Listeners are not mind readers and they can't imagine what we intended if it's not in the song. That's not to imply that every lyric must be literal, or that it must spoon-feed every bit of information to the listener. That's appropriate and desirable for many Pop, Country, and Urban songs. But including every detail of your story in a literal, logical manner might dilute the emotional impact and be inappropriate for some Alternative or Rock songs.

The key is to be sure that you're accomplishing what you intend. If your objective is to have your audience understand exactly what your lyrics mean, you must provide them with sufficient information. Use the tools of effective lyric and melody writing to deliver your message from your heart to theirs.

We songwriters tend to have huge blind spots when it comes to our own creations. To be sure that you're communicating what you think you're expressing, run your songs past people who will be honest with you and get professional feedback whenever possible.

Likewise, if there's something you want to be sure the listener will hear, include it in the song—and on the demo. For example, if you envision a three-part harmony in your choruses, or a catchy guitar lick during your intro, don't assume that anyone else will imagine it. They won't. Be careful to avoid falling into the trap of assuming that your listeners will hear what you intended. If the meaning of your lyric is important to you (and it better be), write it in such a way that it will be clear to your listeners—or you can always write a note and attach it to every CD.

THE HUNGER

I'm writing this at thirty-seven thousand feet in the air, on the plane returning from Los Angeles where I delivered the keynote speech to more than a thousand songwriters at the Taxi Road Rally. (For those who haven't heard of it, Taxi is an independent A&R agency that screens songs and artists for a fee and forwards the best submissions to those individuals and organizations looking for material.)*

It's been many years, but it sometimes seems like just a breath ago that I was living in Los Angeles, struggling to pay my bills, and dreaming that someday I would write a hit song. I'd attended every workshop and class available. Now, I could hardly believe that I was considered "the expert" and was also included on a panel of "Hit Songwriters" next to Lamont Dozier, writer of so many of the Motown hits that were part of the soundtrack of my childhood.

The introduction of each writer on the panel included the playing of snippets of their most successful songs. When Lamont's songs were played ("Stop in the Name of Love," "Heat Wave," "Where Did Our Love Go," etc.) the audience and other panelists erupted into a spontaneous standing ovation that moved Dozier to tears. It was an awesome demonstration of how deeply music touches our lives.

Following my presentations, I spent a total of seven hours autographing copies of my book, 6 *Steps to Songwriting Success: The Comprehensive Guide to Writing and Marketing Hit Songs*, my instructional CDs, and my own CD, *The Way I Heard It*. I had an opportunity to speak with hundreds of aspiring writers that day. Their hunger to achieve success permeated the air and I recognized that hunger all too well.

As I mentioned earlier, following my move to L.A. to become a successful songwriter, more than eleven years passed before I could say that although I didn't earn much money, I earned my living as a songwriter. I had to invest five-and-a-half additional years learning my craft as a staff-writer, earning as little as $10,500 during many of those years,

---

* For additional information, check out **www.Taxi.com**

before I had hit records. During those first years as a professional writer I brought rough work tapes of my new songs to my publisher, who would tear them to shreds.

His suggestions included new angles for second verses, better ways to express my stories, fresher imagery, catchier choruses, more imaginative titles, and so on. He once said, "There's only four things wrong with this song: the melody, the lyrics, the verses, and the chorus!" I'd rewrite and rewrite—and then I'd rewrite my rewrites.

Every time my publisher showed me where my songs had fallen short, I was initially frustrated and terribly disappointed that they weren't as good as I'd hoped and believed. But each time I grasped what was wrong and made it better, not only did I incorporate elements that improved a particular song—I also learned lessons that would become evident in successful songs I'd write years later.

Getting my songs critiqued was a bit like being a pinball. When I'd hit a side bumper (for example, being told my chorus melody wasn't strong enough) and then write a more memorable melody, I'd get pushed toward the center, where I could stay "in play," and have a shot at winning the game. The next time I might hit the other side bumper by writing a lyric that failed to evoke the intended emotion or lacked fresh, detailed imagery. Again, I'd get pushed further back into the center of the action by working hard to correct those areas that had missed the mark.

As my skills improved, sometimes there wouldn't be anything "wrong" with my song. There just wasn't anything exceptional or fresh enough about the idea, melody, or lyric to edge out the competition. In some ways, those were the most frustrating critiques to receive, yet the most helpful. They sent me back to the drawing board with increased determination to write a hit.

It was my hunger for success that kept me going in the face of the seemingly insurmountable odds and the crushing, repeated rejections. That same hunger made it almost unbearable to work at the "day jobs" that kept me from devoting the time and energy I wanted to give to my music. I felt tortured by being kept from writing eight hours a day, and, once home, I was too exhausted to do my best work.

"If only I didn't have to work, I could be a successful writer." Although I didn't know it at the time, the truth was that I needed those years of miserable temp jobs to allow the lessons I was learning about writing to sink in and later emerge in my songs. I hated that hunger, because I translated it into feeling like a failure. Without a staff-writing deal or a hit song on the charts, I felt frustrated, deprived, and miserable much of the time. I've heard these feelings echoed from so many of my students and they hung heavy in the air at the Taxi Road Rally.

Now I look back and I see that hunger as my friend. It was the coach who kept pushing me, and who kept me trudging toward my goal, no matter how impossible that goal seemed to others. It was the force that kept me rewriting and studying my craft, and it was the voice in my heart that whispered I would make it.

The times when I felt like a failure were all parts of the journey to success. I wish I had been kinder and gentler with myself along the way. If I had never written a hit song, the journey would still have been worthwhile. In some ways, following a dream is just as important as having one come true—and I thank the hunger for keeping me on that path.

Exercise

One of the biggest pitfalls developing songwriters fall into is using generic descriptions in their lyrics, instead of creating the specific details that add interest and uniqueness. Instead of using adjectives such as pretty, nice, sexy, kind, beautiful, sweet, or handsome in your songs, try describing what the listener would see if he or she could see the characters as you do. Likewise, when describing a situation, instead of writing, "It was fun," use words that indicate action so the listener will know it was fun.

For example, instead of writing, "He was handsome," you might try to write lines like:

✓ "He's got a body carved like a Greek God."

✓ "His eyes were as blue as a Montana morning sky."

✓ "Heads turn when he walks down the street in those painted-on blue jeans."

✓ "That crooked, chipped-tooth smile lights up his face."

Using color, detail, and action sets your lyric apart and allows the listener to "see" what you see. Try writing specific, vivid descriptions of the following. (Don't worry about rhymes. The purpose of this exercise is simply to practice incorporating detail.)

✓ She's sexy.

✓ He's crazy.

✓ We had a great time.

✓ It was a beautiful place.

✓ He was ugly.

THE PERFECT COLLABORATOR

At a recent workshop a student asked me, "Since you write both melody and lyrics, why do you cowrite?" For me, one of the best reasons is that it keeps me disciplined. If I have a writing appointment scheduled for next Tuesday at 10:00 a.m., it's a safe bet that I'm going to write that day whether I'm "in the mood" or not. Being basically lazy, there's a fair chance that I won't wake up feeling like writing a song. The chances are also good that, by the end of the day, I'll be glad that I wrote and will have grown in some way from the experience, even if the resulting song never becomes a hit.

Another reason to cowrite is that it expands your network of contacts. I've met some of my best collaborators (and friends) through cowriters. I've also been introduced to publishers, record label executives, hit producers, great demo singers, and recording artists by my collaborators. As in any networking situation, you increase your contacts exponentially when you cowrite because you have the potential to access information and make connections, not just from your collaborator, but also from his or her network of collaborators, and their networks of collaborators, on down the line. It's sort of like looking into a series of mirrors and having the images seem to go on forever.

Writing with another writer also gives you instant feedback. It's hard to be objective about our own children. When I suggest a lyric or melodic line to a cowriter who I've learned to trust and she scrunches up her face as if she were smelling chemical waste, I pretty much have the answer I needed. Likewise, if she starts jumping up and down ecstatically. This brings to mind a memorable day I spent writing with British writer/artist Brendan Croker (of the Notting Hillbillies). Brendan is quite an outrageous character, and at one point when I suggested a line, Brendan (wearing a kilt at the time) said with his ever-so-British accent, "Knockers." I wasn't sure if this was a good thing or bad. It turned out to mean that he thought it was quite "smashing."

When I lived in Los Angeles there were times I was so poor I could barely afford food (and if you read my first book you've heard the stories about my eating kitty tuna!). Spending money to record professional demos was out of the question. Back then I defined my ideal collaborator as someone who owned recording equipment and could play all of the instruments. In other words, a ticket to a free demo.

I attended songwriter workshops and specifically sought out cowriters who produced their own demos. I didn't know how else I could have demoed my songs at that point. In retrospect, I can see that neither the songs nor the demos were very good. I was at an early point in my development as a songwriter and so were my collaborators. There were skills that we still needed to acquire and practice. Although those early songs weren't hits, the demos served as a way for me to share my work with other writers and to receive critiques from music industry professionals.

I went through a period in which I concluded that success in the music business is all about who you know. So, I decided that the perfect collaborator would be one who was well connected. For example, if I couldn't write with a hit artist, maybe I could write with his cousin. If I couldn't get a meeting with a publisher, maybe I could open that door by writing with a publisher's assistant—or husband. I didn't have much success doing this because most of these writers were looking to write with writers who were already successful or equally well connected.

So what's the magic answer to the question, "Who is the perfect collaborator?" For me, it's the one who brings something out of me that would not emerge if I were writing alone or with any other writer. When I sit down to write with Karen Taylor-Good, there's an extraordinary chemistry between us. Karen is an amazing artist, and was Grammy nominated for "Country Song of the Year" (for her song, "How Can I Help You Say Goodbye," written with Burton Collins) but I'm not riding on her coattails. There are contributions I've made to melodies and lyrics that I've written with Karen that would never have come out of me if any other writer had been sitting in the room. I've written with hundreds of writers, but I've found that chemistry only a handful of times.

Of course, you have the best chance of a successful collaboration if your skills complement each other's. It probably doesn't make much sense for a writer who is exclusively a lyricist to write with another lyricist—unless there will be a third cowriter who specializes in great melodies. Likewise, two writers who write only melodies are going to have a hard time finishing a song—unless it's an instrumental.

You need to feel comfortable with your cowriter so that you feel safe enough to risk sharing your work in a rough form. You also need to be on the same wavelength. The worst collaboration I've ever experienced was with a writer who's written some of my favorite songs. We're talking classic, great songs and I was honored and excited to write with him. As our song evolved, though, it became painfully clear that we had very different visions for it. I was absolutely certain that we were writing a rowdy, fun, uptempo, country rocker. He was just as equally convinced that we were writing a midtempo, bluesy, Eric Clapton-esque song.

It was obvious that we were never going to agree. I eventually got so disgusted that I said, "Fine. Go ahead and demo the song any way you want." I never spoke to him again and have never pitched the song. But that was a rare bad experience. Throughout the years I've written with hundreds of writers, with varying degrees of success. Most of the collaborations have been positive experiences, even if the songs were less than stellar.

We've all heard the suggestion to "write up," meaning to collaborate with those who have managed to claw their way farther up the food chain. Writing with someone who's higher up the proverbial ladder is like playing tennis with a player who is a little better than you are. It pushes you to do your very best work in order to keep up and usually helps you acquire new skills along the way.

I've learned from experience (like the nightmare I just described) that writing with someone who has had hits does not guarantee that you'll write one together. I've written lots of "good" (but not great) songs with some of the most successful writers in the business. Then again, I've written some of my best songs with writers who had not previously written any hits. Certainly, there is much to gain if you click artistically and do your best work with someone who has more credibility and contacts in the business. Making those connections can be critical.

Writers at every level are looking to write up—so why should someone who's farther along in their career want to write with you? They're probably not going to invest their time and energy just to be "a nice guy." You've got to bring something to the table to attract them, and to keep them there in the future.

Several things might entice potential collaborators. Being well connected is a great way to get successful writers to work with you. I have no doubt that early on the only reason many of my cowriters who were farther up the ladder wrote with me was because I worked in the A&R department at RCA Records. They perceived that working with me would increase the chances of their songs being listened to by the artists on the label. But I don't think they would have continued to write with me if my contribution wasn't adding to our songs. So, if you're lucky enough to have some good connections, be sure you also have mastered the skills to deliver a great song or your credibility will quickly disappear. Having connections is great, but most of us have to rely on other ways to attract successful collaborators.

Typically, the best thing you can offer a potential cowriter is a *great* (not "good") idea presented in a professional manner. In several instances I've worked with songwriting students of mine with no previous track record, because they brought in a title that knocked me out, and they presented it in a way that made me believe that I could write this song with them—and have a hit. When approaching a successful writer with whom you hope to collaborate, don't grovel or act desperate. That's an instant turnoff. If your idea is truly exceptional, you're doing them a favor. In the event they don't choose to write with you, don't take it personally. Ask another successful writer.

If you are an aspiring recording artist with star potential, this may also be a factor that makes successful writers want to collaborate with you. A writer who believes you'll be the next big thing would be wise to work with you before you become a superstar. Be clear about whether you're writing for yourself or to pitch to other artists. If the goal is to write for yourself, be ready to provide samples of your work and the direction of your project.

Critique sessions offer a terrific opportunity to "audition" collaborators. In addition to the educational opportunities, workshops where songs are screened or critiqued provide a built-in chance to listen to songs written by potential collaborators. There's a lot you can learn about writers with whom you're considering working by observing them having their songs critiqued. Not only will you hear the quality of their writing and demos, but you'll also be able to observe their attitude and professionalism. In addition, you'll be able to see the way these writers handle constructive criticism, as well as the extent to which they're open to rewriting.

If you attend writers' nights, workshops, or music industry functions where successful writers are present, you might approach an established writer by saying, "I really enjoy and respect your work and I have an exceptionally strong idea that I'm looking to cowrite. Would you be willing to listen to it?" Many times the answer will be, "No." But occasionally the answer will be, "Sure." You'll probably have more success attracting a collaborator who is one or two notches ahead of you on the ladder than someone who has already earned a Grammy or had Number One singles.

To maximize my chances for a successful collaboration, I come in with several great ideas that I've worked on in advance. I call these "song starts"; they might be titles, melodic hooks, a rough draft of a verse or chorus, a catchy melodic phrase, or snippets of a lyric. I use whatever I bring in as a starting point and seek input and a different perspective from my cowriter. Otherwise, why cowrite?

If you only have one or two ideas, you run the risk of your concept or title being something that doesn't excite your cowriter, bringing your potential collaboration to a quick conclusion. I've had instances where my great, "original" idea was one that my cowriter had previously written. I've had several instances where just in the course of conversation we found an idea we both wanted to write. Stay open to the chemistry between you and the other writer and allow that to dictate the flow.

Like any personal relationship, often the only way to find those "perfect" collaborators is by kissing a lot of frogs. Hopefully, you'll find those cowriters who are a joy for you to work with and who bring out the very best in you.

NOTHING CHANGES IF
NOTHING CHANGES

I didn't want to stop eating fudge brownies, cheesecake, and Haagen-Dazs, and I certainly didn't want to exercise more; I just wanted to weigh less. I didn't want to stop splurging on fancy restaurants, expensive vacations, and new clothes—and I certainly never wanted to trade in my BMW for a Toyota; I just wanted more money in the bank. Things never seem to work the way I want. Life is so unfair.

When I was taking the first steps of my journey as a songwriter, I didn't want to change the way I wrote songs, either. I just wanted my self-indulgent ramblings to be hits on the radio. I was angry and frustrated that my songs weren't bringing me the fame and fortune that I knew I deserved. What was wrong with these publishers? Couldn't they tell how wonderful my songs were?

No, they couldn't tell how wonderful my songs were. I wonder why that was. These were professionals who didn't know me and had no reason to be predisposed to liking or disliking my songs. Gosh, you don't think there might have been something wrong with my songs, do you?

As crazy as this may sound, when I was an aspiring songwriter the possibility that the problem might have laid with the quality of my songs honestly never entered my mind. It's ironic because now that I've had considerable success and acquired an arsenal of songwriting skills and techniques, I'm much more critical of my work. It's easy for me to see why so many of the hits on the radio are hits—and why so many of my songs are not.

Confidence is great, and healthy self-esteem is a terrific asset when pursuing a creative endeavor where rejection is a normal part of the journey. But there's a difference between believing in one's self and being unable to honestly assess the quality of your own work. I've critiqued songs with incomprehensible lyrics and melodies that could barely be considered "melodic." Some of these songs came attached with letters proclaiming them to be "the next Number One smash hit." I've also written more than my share of those songs. When I wrote them, I saw them as perfect, just as any parent sees his or her child as the most beautiful and cleverest baby in the world.

The inability of some developing writers to assess their own work is truly an amazing phenomenon. It's true that "d'Nile" is not just a river in Egypt. Most songwriters seem to think that their latest creation is the best they've ever done. I suspect that as artists, we need to believe that each new project we're working on is truly extraordinary in order to summon enough energy to push our "baby" through the birth process and then expose it to the world. Alas, most babies are only average. And, let's face it, some are truly ugly. The good news is that, as songwriters, we don't have a moral or legal obligation to love, nurture, and pay to put each one of our creations through college. We can file some of them away, learn our lessons, and move on to the next song. *But this is something we'll be likely to do only if we accept that every song we write is not necessarily perfect.*

It seems like a paradox. I treat each new song and demo as if it were the one that could change my life, as if the success of my entire career is riding on getting that one line of lyric or melody just right. With a lower standard I wouldn't stand a chance of successfully competing in such a cutthroat business. Yet the truth is that only a fraction of the songs that I put so much of my heart and soul into will ever be recorded. Even fewer of them will generate income. I've read that the "average" professional songwriter (there's an oxymoron for you) typically earns royalties from only five percent of his or her songs.

We couldn't give a thousand percent to each song if we didn't believe that it could be "the one." We need to do everything in our power to make each song we write the best one we've ever written, and we need to believe that it is—at least until the next one comes along.

WHY GIVE AWAY HALF YOUR MONEY?

A talented, aspiring songwriter who had attended several of my workshops recently sent me a letter expressing his frustration over the difficulty he's having trying to find a music publisher to represent his songs. He said he was considering placing his songs with on-line services where those looking for material could listen. He was also thinking about subscribing to "tip sheets" (listings of artists who are looking for songs to record), as well as establishing his own publishing company. He added that by taking these actions he would not only avoid the time and energy he'd been investing in searching for a publisher, he'd make twice as much money. He asked for my opinion and some of my thoughts about this follow.

I empathize with what this writer was feeling. My mind drifted back to a period of several years that I'd almost forgotten about. While living in Los Angeles, I was so frustrated by my inability to secure a publisher to represent my songs that I decided to take on that role myself. I bought a cassette duplicator (in the days before CDs) and had letterhead, cassette labels, and mailing labels printed with my company name. I changed the message on my answering machine to sound like a place of business and, suddenly, I became a publisher.

After long hours of working my "day job," I'd come home, take a quick nap, and then research which record labels, producers, and artists were currently looking for songs. I'd find this information by reading trade papers and the tip sheets that I subscribed to, by networking with other songwriters, and by calling the record labels directly. I'd frequently work well past midnight typing cover letters and address labels, copying lyric sheets, and making tape copies. Over a period of several years I spent a considerable amount of money (for demos, postage, envelopes, and blank cassettes), time, and energy pitching songs that weren't competitive. Of course I didn't know that at the time—and nothing anyone could have said or done would have convinced me that my songs were less than hits. Needless to say, I never got any positive results. Was it all a waste of time? I don't think so. It was a part of my journey and I learned some valuable lessons.

In retrospect, I can see that my time would have been better spent honing my songwriting skills and networking to find a publisher who might have represented my songs and helped me develop into a better, more successful writer. As they say, hindsight is 20/20.

Before further examining the pros and cons of being your own publisher, it'll be beneficial to describe what music publishing entails. For most developing songwriters, being offered an opportunity to publish their songs is analogous to finding the Holy Grail. Being a "published songwriter" sounds like the pinnacle of success, but that's not necessarily the case.

When a book, poem, or magazine article is published, the work appears in print and is typically available for sale. However, having a song published simply means that an individual or company agrees to act as your agent, that is, to use their best efforts to generate income from the song. Many writers are shocked to learn that part of what "publishing" typically means includes assigning fifty percent of any income their song might earn to the publisher. Unless the song is recorded by a successful recording artist, included in a film or television show, or sold as sheet music, there won't be any income for either the writer or publisher. The overwhelming majority of published songs never earn a dime.

All income derived from songwriting royalties is split equally between the "writer's" share and the "publisher's" share. So, for every dollar earned, fifty cents goes to the writer and fifty cents to the publisher. If a writer has not assigned his or her publishing rights to another company or individual, then he or she owns both the writer's share as well as the publisher's share of any income that song might generate.*

I sometimes hear aspiring writers boast that they'll make twice as much money because they're opening their own publishing company and retaining their publishing share (which is usually referred to as "the publishing"). Establishing a publishing company is easy to do. You start by reserving a name from the performing rights organization (PRO) of your choice. In the United States your only options are ASCAP (the American Society of Composers, Authors, and Publishers), BMI (Broadcast Music International), or SESAC (formerly known as Society of European Stage Authors and Composers, now simply called SESAC). Next, you fill out a few simple forms, enclose a check, print up some letterhead on your computer, and "Poof"—you're a publisher.

By the way, the primary function of PROs is to collect and distribute royalties earned for radio airplay, television broadcasts, and performances of music in venues such as restaurants, nightclubs, airplanes, shopping malls, and roller rinks. If your songs are

---

* For a more detailed discussion of songwriting royalties, publishing, and performing rights organizations, see Step V, "Taking Care of Business," in 6 *Steps to Songwriting Success* (Billboard Books).

being played on the radio, on television, or in these other venues, you must be a member of one of the PROs to collect your performance royalties as a writer or publisher.

Bear in mind that a publisher must be affiliated with the same PRO as the writer it represents. So, for instance, if you are signed with BMI as a writer, your publishing company must be a BMI company. That's why large publishing companies that sign writers affiliated with different PROs are actually comprised of several subsidiaries. For example, Warner/Chappell Music owns WB Music Corp. to collect performance royalties generated by its ASCAP-affiliated writers; Warner-Tamerlane Publishing Corp. for its BMI-affiliated writers; and W.B.M. Music Corp. for its writers who are members of SESAC.

So, if it's that easy to become a publisher, why would I want to give away half of my royalties by allowing someone else to publish my songs? Well, the simple answer is that earning fifty percent of significant income is preferable to one hundred percent of nothing. For example, while it's true that my publisher earned hundreds of thousands of dollars from my songs recorded by Britney Spears and the Backstreet Boys, so did I—and this is income that never would have been generated without my publisher's connections. (Zomba owned Jive Records, the label that Britney and the Backstreet Boys were signed to, at the time when these artists recorded my songs.)

In the olden days, a publisher's primary function was to print and market sheet music. Back in the days before CDs, cassettes, and other forms of recorded music, sheet music sales used to be where the bulk of a songwriter's income came from. Music lovers would buy a copy of the sheet music of the latest hit song and learn to play it on their piano. Today, making sheet music available is a very small part of a publisher's job. Unless a song is a major hit, with the exception of some choral and religious music, there will be no customers for its sheet music.

Today, a publisher's primary task is to generate income from sales and performance royalties. This happens by placing songs with recording artists. In order to facilitate getting songs recorded, successful publishers develop the contacts necessary to get meetings with artists and those individuals in charge of helping artists find songs to record (i.e., A&R representatives at record labels, producers, and artists' managers).** They also arrange collaborations between their writers and other successful writers, artists, and producers. These collaborations often provide a more direct route to getting songs recorded than simply pitching them to record labels, artists, or producers.

In addition to their administrative functions, good publishers provide feedback and creative input for their writers. Having a professional, objective opinion can really help make our songs the best they can be. When deciding whether being your own publish-

---

** Many publishers also have divisions that work to place songs in films and TV shows.

er is the best route for you, assess whether you can fulfill these functions as well as a professional publisher would be able to.

While anyone can mail a CD to a record label or producer, unless you're an established "name" publisher or writer, it's typically not effective to pitch songs this way. You'll find that many companies will either return the songs as "unsolicited" or will never listen to them. It's much more common for songs to be placed as a result of being played at a face-to-face meeting with a music business professional.

When I was a struggling songwriter, paying my rent by screening songs for RCA Records and, later, handling production coordination for albums by Country stars including Aaron Tippin, I rarely took the time to wade through the piles of tapes from unknown writers and publishers. That's not to say there couldn't have been a good song in the bunch. However, since my time was limited, I felt I had a better chance of finding that elusive "hit" if I first listened to songs that had come from successful writers and established publishing companies. Unfortunately, I rarely had the time to listen beyond that first tier.

In my experience, and that of the students I've worked with, it's incredibly difficult for a writer without a track record to make a mark in the music business without the representation and credibility of a publisher. While any reputable pitch sheet (such as *RowFax* or *SongLink*) will tell you who's looking for songs, mailing your CD won't necessarily get it listened to. It's rare that a cut happens that way. This business is about personal relationships—and that's where a publisher comes in.

If your songs are at a level where legitimate publishers would be willing to represent them, but you *choose* to be your own publisher, that's a valid choice—presuming you have the business savvy, desire, and skills necessary to successfully market your material. Don't be discouraged if one or two publishers fail to get excited about your songs. That's par for the course. But if you've received a half dozen or more rejections from reputable publishers, there's probably a good reason why they don't feel they can get your songs recorded.

To summarize, my take is that your time is best spent developing your songwriting skills and seeking a reputable publisher to represent your songs. Sure, it's easier and less frustrating in the short term to avoid a certain amount of rejection by being your own publisher. But, it's tough to get a song cut and, generally, if you try hard and still can't find a publisher to represent your songs, then it's doubtful you'd be able to get those same songs recorded by pitching them yourself.

I don't have a crystal ball, and I don't claim to have all the answers. There are no "rules" in the music business, and if you search hard enough you could probably find an exception to each and every thing that I teach. Follow your own path. If your heart tells you to be your own publisher, go for it. But if what you really want is to have a legitimate publisher recognize and represent your songs, continue to work on your songwriting.

Remember that success in this business is based on writing *exceptional* songs—not good ones. That's not easy to do. I haven't found any shortcuts, quick answers, or guarantees. But I can promise that with practice, patience, and perseverance you'll have a better chance of writing the kinds of songs that make publishers take notice.

SETTING REALISTIC GOALS

**"If you don't know where you are going,
you might end up someplace else."**
                              —Yogi Berra

It's 10:40 a.m. By this evening, more than anything in the world, I would like to have a Top Ten single on the charts. Gosh, if I had only woken up a little earlier—like five years ago!

It's important to set goals and to achieve them. We need those little successes along the way to show us that we're on the right track. They keep our spirits up in the face of the inevitable rejection that's part of the deal when we pursue creative endeavors.

But setting goals that are virtually impossible to attain is counterproductive. It's true that if we set our sights on the stars, even if we never reach them, we'll see the beauty of the sky. For most of us, though, it's easy to feel that those stars are so many light years away that there's no point in aiming for them—we'll never reach them anyway.

So what can I accomplish *today?* I can't write a book, secure a recording contract, or get a song on the charts by this evening. These goals all take time. Just like losing weight, short of cutting off a limb I can't lose twenty pounds by Tuesday. On the other hand, if I follow a healthy food plan and exercise regularly, I have a great probability of losing that weight a little at a time over the next several months. If I'm willing to stick to that plan, there's a great chance that I'll maintain my goal weight long-term. Similarly, it would be great to have a rock-solid muscular body. Unfortunately, that would require working out, lifting weights, and taking other actions that I loathe and am not willing to do.

Wouldn't it be bliss if the key to losing weight and having the perfect body was lying in a recliner, watching TV, taking naps, and eating pizza? It doesn't work that way in the real world. Deal with it. Success in any creative endeavor requires hard work and doing some things most of us would probably rather not do. I need to decide how badly I want what I want. What sacrifices am I willing to make?

I need to look at what I can accomplish today and what goals and commitments I can establish over the next several months and beyond. Okay, so I can't write the best song of my career, record a professional demo, get it recorded, released, watch it sail up the charts, and win a Grammy before lunch. But I can work an hour this afternoon on a rewrite and make a couple of phone calls to gather information about recording a demo.

I can make a commitment to working on my songs, as well as on the business side of my career, for one hour each morning before going to work and for three hours on Tuesday and Thursday evenings. I can join a songwriters' organization, plan on attending a song camp next summer, work on a creative exercise for twenty minutes, explore resources on the Internet, set an appointment to collaborate, or practice playing a new song on the guitar.

No matter how badly I want them, there are some goals that I will not achieve immediately. Looking back, it's clear that all the baby steps I took when it seemed like my dreams were impossible to reach somehow added up. The years went by while I was busy working on my goals and, incredible as it still seems, many of those dreams came true. There's so much more I hope to achieve, and I may not accomplish everything I hope to in this lifetime. There are only so many hours in the day—and only so many days. But I've learned from experience that when I set my sights on my goals, set a course, and stick to my game plan, sometimes dreams really do come true.

Exercise

Take a moment to think about what commitments you're willing to make for your career today.

- ✓ On a sheet of paper, write down what you hope to accomplish in the next thirty days.
- ✓ Then list those actions you are willing to commit to in order to achieve your goal.
- ✓ Now write about what you hope to accomplish in the upcoming three months, six months, and one year.
- ✓ Again, list those actions that you can realistically commit to that will help lead you to accomplish your goals.
- ✓ Share your goals with a "buddy." You can support and encourage each other to fulfill your promises to your careers. Set a time each week to check in and report that you have indeed taken the actions you've committed to.

NOW WHAT?

Let's presume you've now reached a point where you can write perfectly crafted songs. Your songs all fit into one of the structures typically heard on the radio. Your lyrics communicate exactly what you intend and include rhymes in all the right places. They fit the music beautifully, incorporate detail and imagery, and clearly tell your story. Your melodies are memorable. They include catchy rhythms and lots of repetition. You're producing competitive demos that sound as good as those being pitched by the pros. Maybe you've even won several song competitions. So, why aren't you having hits? Why are you still working a miserable day job? And what do you need to do to get to that next level?

This situation reminds me of a turning point in my career. After more than five years of attending every available workshop, studying the songwriting books, and honing my craft every night after work, I had an appointment with Rodney Gordy, who at the time was a publisher at Motown's Jobete Music. I planned to play Rodney a new song that I was sure had the greatest hit potential of any one I'd written to date.

Not only did I think this song was terrific, but it was the best-sounding demo I'd ever produced. I'd bitten the bullet and hired a professional demo singer whom I couldn't afford, telling myself that I couldn't afford *not* to have the best available vocalist. My hope was that Rodney would offer to publish the song. My fantasy was that he'd be so impressed that right on the spot he'd offer me a staff-writing deal—an exclusive songwriting agreement that comes with a monetary advance. I wanted that deal more than anything in the world. Being a staff-writer would be my ticket to quitting my day job and having the time, professional support, and resources to do what I was always meant to do: write songs.

I knew how good this song was and I couldn't imagine his turning it down. I was totally unprepared when he casually said he'd pass. When I asked if he could offer any feedback that might help, he stated that there was nothing wrong with the song. He said I'd written a "staff-writer" song; one that was just as good, *but not better than or significantly different from* those songs that any one of his staff-writers could produce on any given day. I left the meeting angry and frustrated. If I was writing at the same level as his staff-writers, why wasn't I one of them?

Over time I came to understand that essentially what I had been told was that I'd crafted a well-written song that wasn't a "hit." There wasn't anything truly *exceptional* about my song; there was nothing in the concept, melody, or lyric to compel an artist, producer, record label executive, or publisher to choose mine over the stiff competition.

What should you do if you're writing staff-writer songs instead of hits? The first thing to do is to congratulate yourself for reaching this level. You've worked hard to get there, and many aspiring writers never master the tools and techniques as well as you already have. You can't get to the next level until you've reached this one, so you're right on track.

Now, let's look at some cold, hard facts. It's not uncommon for a major artist to be pitched in the ballpark of 1,200 songs for his or her album. Most of these songs will have been written by professional writers with major credits. There are simply not enough slots on hit albums to accommodate every songwriter who's vying for one of them.

If an album includes twelve songs, it's likely that some of them will be "inside" songs: those written or cowritten by the artist, producer, label executive's boyfriend, or someone else involved in the project. It's likely that a couple of the songs will be contributed by one of a handful of top writers who are consistent hit-makers. This may leave only one or two available slots.

How can you possibly compete? Nashville publisher John Van Meter said, "Every cut is a miracle," and I'd have to agree. Then how *do* you cut through the competition?

You've got to give the listener (a publisher, producer, record label executive, or recording artist) a compelling reason to choose your song over all the other songs in consideration, including those that may have been written by the artist. That reason won't be your sparkling personality; it will be a combination of a fresh, unique lyric, an attention-grabbing idea, an exceptional melody, and a demo that shows off the song to its best advantage. In other words, as I've said earlier, in a field this competitive, "good" isn't good enough.

Let's assume you've indeed written a truly incredible song. Now other factors come into play. The publisher you meet with may already be representing other songs that are similar to yours. He may have thirty staff-writers he's already committed to. Possibly your song is not to his personal taste, or maybe he's just having a bad day and missed the fact that your song truly is brilliant. Presuming your songs really are strong, there are a multitude of reasons why a given publisher might choose not to publish them. And those reasons may have little or nothing to do with the quality of your writing.

If you're targeting huge publishing corporations that have tens of thousands of songs in their catalog, as well as fifty or more staff-writers (many with Number One songs to their credit), there's not much of a chance that your song will be something they feel they "need." However, if you're pitching to a publisher who represents a small catalog of songs and does not have a commitment to many staff-writers, your song (if it's exceptional) will likely be something this publisher will be thrilled to represent. Developing writers often achieve their initial successes by working with small, independent publishing companies.

There are countless stories of songs that went on to become huge hits after being rejected by virtually every record label. "Change My Mind" was rejected more than seventy-five times before becoming a single for The Oak Ridge Boys. The single stiffed and it was an additional five years and one hundred more rejections before the song became a Top Five Country single for John Berry.

Each time my song was rejected, did that mean that it was a "bad" song? Was each rejection proof of my greatest fear—that I had no talent? Apparently not, but each rejection felt like it came with the message that I wasn't good enough and would never be successful. As songwriters, we're regularly called upon to bare our souls while maintaining the skin thickness of an armadillo.

Timing is another critical factor. It won't matter how perfect your song is for Faith Hill if Faith just finished recording her album. It will be at least an additional nine months, or even a year, before her record label and producer are seriously looking for songs. Even if you were able to get a song through to her and she placed it on "hold," by the time she's ready to record there's a good chance that your song will be replaced by a new, exciting find or that she may be looking for a different type of material.

Once the demo goes into the mail, there are at least a thousand factors that are out of our control. We can't affect the mood the listener will be in when he or she hears the song; whether it will fit a specific slot required for a particular project; whether the idea of our song is similar to one the artist has already recorded for this album; if it's consistent with a theme or concept for the album; whether it's something a particular artist wants to express musically and lyrically; or hundreds of other things that might stand between us and getting this song recorded by this artist.

So, what can you do? Keep plugging away. Hone your skills until you can consistently write excellent songs—and, occasionally, exceptional ones. Build your catalog until you have incredible, fresh songs that are appropriate for a wide variety of artists. Continue to network, join local songwriting organizations, and attend workshops and seminars where you'll have an opportunity to interact with industry professionals and other writers who are working their way up the ladder. Understand that it's normal for a song to face many rejections before finding its home. And remember, you've chosen to pursue a career in a fiercely competitive field. Don't beat yourself up for not being where you'd like to be. You're on your way.

YOU CAN'T BE SUCCESSFUL
BECAUSE . . .

I'd been living in Los Angeles for several months when my father came to visit. Since I was living in a cockroach- and mouse-infested room and sharing a communal bathroom with the sordid characters who lived in the other rooms, my father wisely decided to stay at a nearby motel on Sunset Boulevard. He was amazed at how friendly all of the attractive young men and women were. Several of them would say, "Hello," and strike up conversations each time he went out for his walk. It didn't occur to him that these were prostitutes! But that's another story . . .

I was anxious to show my father all that I was doing to pursue my dream of becoming a professional songwriter. I hoped he'd emotionally support my decision to leave my job and family in Philadelphia to follow my heart and seek success in the music business in L.A. So, I took Dad to a workshop sponsored by the Songwriters' Guild of America (SGA).

Each month, the workshop featured a different guest who shared his or her experience. The aspiring songwriters hung on every word. This particular month, the speakers were Jay Livingston and Ray Evans. These two old-timers had written classics including "Que Sera, Sera," "Mona Lisa," the theme song to the television show *Mr. Ed*, and many more hits.

Livingston and Evans sat at the piano and shared wonderful stories about how some of their biggest hits had come to be written and recorded. I especially enjoyed the story of how they rewrote their Christmas standard, "Silver Bells," from its original title, "Tinkle Bells." They played snippets of their songs to illustrate their points as I sat in the audience, imagining that someday I'll have written hit songs, too. As my father and I left the workshop, he casually said, "You can't be a successful songwriter because you don't play piano."

Well, I was furious. My anger rose partly because he was punching a hole in my fragile dream, partly because I interpreted his statement to mean that he didn't believe in my talent, and partly because it probably hit much too close to my own fears, which I didn't want to acknowledge.

We argued and I tried to convince him that there was a world of difference between the ability to play a musical instrument and being able to write hit melodies and lyrics. I had moved three thousand miles from my family and friends, ended a relationship, and traded a secure job and a comfy middle-class existence for poverty. I guess I was also trying hard to convince myself.

Time has proven my father wrong. I've written the lyrics *and* melodies for hit songs without ever having learned to play the piano—and my guitar-playing skills still lie somewhere between pitiful and mediocre. Perhaps you're a terrific pianist or guitarist and perhaps you've been extensively trained in musical theory. If so, don't despair. If you look hard enough, you'll be sure to find at least a thousand more reasons why you can't possibly be successful.

Take your pick and feel free to add your own excuses to this list:

"I can't carry a tune in a bucket."

"I'm too old."

"I have no musical training."

"I'm too young."

"I have too much classical musical training."

"I have to work a 'day job'."

"No one in my family has ever been musical."

"I have three kids demanding my attention."

"I have no money to produce demos."

"I wouldn't know where to start."

"I'm too shy to sing."

"But I live in the middle of Iowa."

And, my personal favorite: "The odds are a million to one. Why should I think I'm so special?"

You can choose to believe any or all of the excuses listed above. Or, you can find solutions to each obstacle. *You don't have time?* How about waking up thirty minutes earlier three days a week? *You have to work a day job?* So did almost every person who's currently a successful songwriter. *You've got kids?* Even God took a day off. I bet you can find someone to watch the little rugrats once or twice a week.

But what about: *The odds are a million to one. Why should I think I'm so special?* Yes, the odds are tough, but you *are* special. No one else in the world can imagine and write the way you can.

Instead of investing your energy in reasons why you can't possibly be successful, make a decision to live your dream. There's no guarantee of success, but you deserve the chance to try.

Exercise

Make a list of all the reasons why you feel you can't be successful. Allow those voices in your head to be as negative as they want to be. This is their chance to express themselves.

You're a creative person, so begin looking for creative ways around each and every obstacle that appears to be in your way. You'll find solutions—if you want them badly enough.

RE-WRITING

WARNING: I'm about to give away the wonderful surprise ending of the film *The Sixth Sense*. If you haven't seen the film and still want to, go rent the movie and revisit this chapter later.

I was stunned to read an interview with writer/director M. Night Shyamalan in which he said that when writing *The Sixth Sense*, he did not get the idea that the psychologist (Bruce Willis' character) was dead *until the fifth draft of his script*. Prior to that, he was simply writing a story about a psychologist working with a boy who sees dead people.

If you've seen the film, you know that the fact that the psychologist is dead is the essence of the film. Without this surprise plot twist, instead of being a critical and financial blockbuster, *The Sixth Sense* would have been just another horror flick about a kid who sees dead people. Nominated for six Oscars, including "Best Picture," and ranked as the Number Ten domestic moneymaker of all time, without the really unique angle of the guy actually being dead, this film would likely have succumbed to the same fate that Shyamalan's previous two films suffered. (Oh, you didn't know he'd written two previous films? That's exactly my point.)

So, what happened? Shyamalan didn't settle for his first, second, third, or even fourth draft of the script. And when you're writing songs, if you want to write the very best you're capable of, you can't either. What's the chance that the very first words that come out of your pen and the very first melody that you create are perfect, that you couldn't possibly improve even one word or one note of what you've written? Sounds unlikely to me.

For a moment, let's forget about commercial success and the prospect of sharing your work with an audience and assume these are not your goals when you create. If your motivation for expressing your creativity is exclusively to experience the intrinsic joy in the process of creating, that's terrific. It's a perfectly valid and wonderful reason to pursue any creative outlet. I hope you'll never stop and never lose the joy it brings. If you fit into this category of "Those-Who-Create-Simply-for-the-Fun-of-It" and you have no desire to expose your work to an audience, you can probably skip ahead to the next chapter.

When we choose to share our artistic creations, whether they are visual works of art, songs, or prose, our hope is to connect with our audience; to evoke a feeling; to reach their hearts. It doesn't matter whether your audience is made up of your best friend or thirty million radio listeners. When we write a joyous piece of dance music, if we've done our job effectively, it will inspire our listeners to want to dance. A song that successfully communicates causes the listeners to feel whatever emotions we intended to evoke.

Songwriter/playwright Mike Reid addressed this beautifully at the NSAI (Nashville Songwriters Association International) Song Camp where we taught together. Reid explained that a common pitfall for developing songwriters is the huge discrepancy between what the writer intends to express and what the audience actually receives, musically as well as lyrically. He stretched his left hand out from his side and explained, "This is what the writer thinks she's expressing." Then he stretched his right hand out from his side and said, "This is what the audience hears." He said that the only way to have the writer's intent and what he or she actually expresses become one and the same is to write many, many songs and receive feedback on your work.

By the way, I was amazed to learn that Mike Reid and Allan Shamblin's classic song, "I Can't Make You Love Me" (made popular by Bonnie Raitt), began its life as an uptempo song that the writers envisioned for Country/Bluegrass star Ricky Skaggs. It was through the process of rewriting that the final heart-wrenching version emerged.

It's difficult to know how our communication is being received without getting feedback, and it's certainly not pleasant if we learn that our listeners had no idea what we meant. But there's no other way to know if we're evoking the emotions and expressing the story that we planned. When we learn that we haven't quite gotten our idea across the way we hoped we had, it's time to rewrite.

My entire career may be the result of having rewritten a particular song *seven times*. At the urging of publisher Jim Vellutato, my cowriter Bryan Cumming and I rewrote (and re-demoed) our song, "I Had a Heart," over and over. Each time that we went back to the drawing board we incorporated more of the publisher's suggestions. In some of those instances we tweaked a melody line. Other times, we tried a new lyrical angle or incorporated a fresher image. Every time we learned that there was still additional work to do, it was initially frustrating and disappointing. But, with each subsequent rewrite, the song was getting better and better.

When Jim finally felt we had made the song as strong as it could be, he Fed Ex'd it to his company's Nashville office. The next afternoon, I received a call notifying me that "I Had a Heart" had been recorded by a new artist named Darlene Austin. Later that year, Darlene was nominated by the Academy of Country Music as "Best New Female Artist of the Year." At that point in my journey, I had neither previously published any of my songs nor had any recorded.

"I Had a Heart" peaked at #63 on the *Billboard* Country Singles chart—and at #46 in Cashbox. From a short-term, financial perspective, the success of that song was minimal. But it provided me with some of the greatest thrills of my life, including the first time I heard a song I'd written played on the radio, saw it performed on television, and saw my name on the *Billboard* charts. Having that song recorded gave me a whole new level of credibility and was a tangible milestone that kept me fired up and plugging away.

Looking back, I can see that it lead to a chain of events that clearly laid the foundation for my entire career. If I had said, "I'm tired of this. I like the song the way it is. What's this jerk know anyway?" and stopped rewriting after the third or fourth version, I wonder how differently my life would have unfolded.

It's never been easy for me to have my songs torn apart, but it's been worth it. I'd rather have my ego squashed today and have a big hit tomorrow, than think my songs are great and never get them recorded. The good news is that as we internalize the critiques we receive throughout the years, it becomes easier to avoid those same mistakes. We get better at recognizing the strengths and weaknesses in our work and can sometimes anticipate what responses we might get from an objective, knowledgeable reviewer.

But no matter how successful we become, we still sometimes need an outside opinion to know if we're hitting the target. Note: your girlfriend, mother, uncle, father-in-law, dentist, and other assorted friends and relatives are *not* typically able to provide constructive criticism. Unless your family and friends are music publishers, successful record producers, or otherwise qualified, it's unlikely that you'll receive much more than, "It sounds like it should be on the radio," when that may not exactly be the case.

Rewriting applies not only to our lyrics, but also to those melodies that are the vehicles that deliver our messages to our listeners' hearts. Using tried and true skills and techniques, receiving feedback, and then rewriting, rewriting, and rewriting are the keys to expressing ourselves creatively in ways that can transcend our own hearts to touch others. Isn't that what you want?

Most writers accept that they'll have to rewrite their lyrics in order to get them right. But then many of them settle for the very first melody that pops into their heads. Melody is not secondary to a song; it's crucial. It's not the words that people walk down the street humming. Crafting the strongest melody you're capable of is not just the result of luck, chance, or God-given talent. There are specific techniques that can be learned and honed to help you rewrite your melodies.*

Remember, it took M. Night Shyamalan five drafts to uncover the key that allowed his script to enter so many hearts and become a box office smash hit. What are the magic elements in your lyric and melody that will set them apart? Have you stopped looking before you've found them? Might you be just one more rewrite away from everything you've dreamed of?

Exercise

Take a good look at a song you've recently finished. Put each line of lyric under the microscope. Even though you like it "as is," just for the purposes of this exercise, rewrite your verse lyrics. Then look over your chorus lyrics and see if there's not even one word you might improve.

Now repeat this process, rewriting your verse and chorus melodies. Try at least five different melodies for each section before deciding which one is your favorite. Remember that if you don't prefer your rewrite, you can always go back to your original version.

---

* For an in-depth discussion of melody techniques, refer to Step III, "Composing Memorable Melodies," in 6 *Steps to Songwriting Success* and the instructional CD, *Writing Hit Melodies with Jason Blume* (Moondream Music).

GET IT TOGETHER

Several of my cowriters have remarked that I seem exceptionally well organized and they've asked how I keep track of all of my melodic and lyric ideas, as well as songs that are works in progress. The truth is that my natural inclination is to have snippets of melodies on unlabeled cassettes and lyrics in a dozen different notebooks. I did that for years and I don't even want to think about how many ideas fell through the cracks and were lost forever.

Like so many things in life, I only changed what I was doing when the fact that it was not working hit me right in the face. On a Monday, I might begin "song number one" and fill ten pages of my notebook with lyrics, images, lines, and thoughts that relate to this song. Tuesday, I'd repeat the process with "song number two." The following week I might get a great idea for the bridge in "song number three" that I'd started the previous week, and that would go on the next empty page of my notebook—possibly twenty pages away from the rest of the lyrics for this song.

After a few weeks had gone by, my notebook would be full of lyrics, many of which were still in progress. So I'd buy a new notebook (which was always exciting because it represented a fresh start and the hope that some of those blank pages might soon be filled with songs that could become my biggest successes).

Now flash forward a few months. I had twenty-five or thirty lyrics in various stages of development, some of which I was wise enough to abandon after working on them for twenty minutes. These lyrics were in a half-dozen or more different spiral-bound notebooks and legal pads. I had a writing appointment to revisit "song number one." Now the problem was that I couldn't find all of my notes. I think that song was begun while I was working with my dark blue spiral notebook, and I could have sworn that the new idea for my second verse came while I was using the yellow legal pad. I was pretty sure that the killer line that hit me for the chorus while I was eating tacos at *Las Manitas* was on a greasy napkin somewhere at the bottom of my suitcase.

I reached a point where I was carrying a half-dozen notebooks with me and spending the first twenty minutes of my writing sessions flipping through pages. "But I'm positive I had a great line to tie up the chorus. I know I'll find it..." When I finally couldn't stand it anymore, I got organized.

Now, when I start working on a new song I bring an empty manila file folder with me to the writing session. At the end of the day all of my lyrics and notes that pertain to this song go into the file folder and I write the name of the song on the tab. I always write in pen and I never erase anything. Paper is cheap, and I never know when I might want to go back and use some of those old ideas. It's not uncommon for me to have twenty or more pages of notes for one song.

Likewise, a cassette with any melodic ideas related to this song goes into the file. This cassette will also contain a rough version, a "work tape" of the song. I typically flip over to side "B" and record my work tape at the beginning of the cassette so I can easily find it when I need to. If I plan to continue working on this song in the next week or so, the folder stays in my briefcase. Otherwise, it goes into a file labeled "Works in Progress" in my home office. When the song is completed and a demo has been recorded, the file, with one hundred percent of my notes and melodic ideas for this song, gets retired to the "Finished Song" file in the basement.

Snippets of both lyric and melodic ideas that I have not yet developed have their own home. Being a positive thinker, I put these cassettes and scraps of paper into a file marked "Future Hits"; this file stays in my briefcase. I label the cassettes that contain my melodic starts with phrases that will help me remember what's on them. For example, one cassette label might read: "Uptempo R&B chorus; Country ballad; quirky Latin-type Dance/Pop, etc."

I periodically go through those matchbook covers, ATM receipts, backs of business cards, and other assorted scraps of paper that hold my lyric ideas and enter them into my computer. I compile and print them so that when a cowriter and I are sharing ideas, looking for the one that will excite and inspire both of us, I have only a few sheets of paper to look through. FYI, I leave several inches between my entries so I'll have room to add notes and additional lines, phrases, or images as they hit me.

Life is much easier now that I'm not frantically flipping through countless notebooks and scraps of paper for my song ideas. My time is better spent writing songs rather than searching for them.

FULL CIRCLE

At a recent BMI (Broadcast Music International) Nashville Songwriters' Workshop that I taught, my special guest was Mike Sebastian, one of Nashville's top music publishers. Back when my dreams were much better developed than my songs, Mike was the first publisher I ever met with in Nashville.

During my lecture portion of the workshop, I focused on those tools and techniques that help us craft melodies that stick in listeners' brains. We listened to examples of hit songs, dissecting them to discover those melodic techniques that contributed to their success. We observed that there were indeed certain elements that were consistently found in various genres including Pop, Country, and R&B.

I talked about the benefit of using repetition, repetition, and repetition. We practiced rhythmic repetition—repeating the same rhythm while changing the actual notes. We crafted a melody by repeating the same melodic phrase exactly, and then tried the same technique while changing the accompanying chords. We noted that short melodic phrases were easier to remember and sing than longer, more complicated ones. We listened to and analyzed hit songs, and noted that these tools had been used in almost all of them.

We examined a variety of ways to break long melodic phrases into shorter segments that were easier to sing. We rewrote melodies by trying a variety of different rhythms. We tried crafting melodies based on ascending and descending melodic phrases. We noted that the hits we studied maintained listener interest by varying the rhythms in the different sections of the song (i.e., verse, chorus, and bridge).

I reminded the participants that there were reasons why certain melodies were "catchier," and that the skills necessary to craft them could be acquired with hard work, practice, and perseverance.* I urged the students to learn the basic tools, but then to push the envelope. We spoke about the necessity of giving the publishers, producers,

---

* An in-depth examination of the melodic techniques and tools mentioned here, plus many more, can be heard on the instructional CD *Writing Hit Melodies with Jason Blume*.

and recording artists the kinds of melodies that would compel them to choose our songs instead of those written by our competition. We noted that each of the songs that had won awards at the recent CMA (Country Music Association) awards show indeed had something special that separated them from the pack.

Following my lecture, when Mike Sebastian, our guest publisher, arrived for his portion of the seminar, I asked him what he looked for in songs and what these developing songwriters would need to do in order to grab his attention. He couldn't have reinforced my lesson any better if I had scripted his response. His answer was, "Be original. Be creative."

Each student had an opportunity to pitch one song to Mike. Most of the songs were good and I beamed with pride like a proud papa. My students had worked hard to master the basics. Our guest publisher held on to seven songs that he wanted to revisit. That was about one out of every five that he'd listened to. For the songs that didn't get chosen, Mike's main comments were that the songs were very well crafted; there was nothing "wrong" with them, but they were just not special enough to make him believe he could take them to meetings and get them cut over the competition.

Mike went above and beyond the call of duty, being exceptionally generous with his time and comments. While it was a terrific learning experience for all those who attended, when Mike's portion was over I was left with a room of mostly very disappointed writers (except for seven whose feet were barely touching the ground). This had been their chance to impress a major publisher, possibly get their first song published, have an open door, and hopefully establish the roots of a long-term relationship.

I could really feel for them because I had been in their shoes for so many years. I know how it felt to get my hopes up and believe with all my heart that a certain meeting or connection would be the one that would change my life forever. I also know how it felt to be devastated when the next day came and I had to return to a job that I detested.

At my workshops, I often share my belief that the fact that you may not be where you want to be professionally today doesn't preclude the possibility of acquiring the skills, tools, and connections that can get you to where you hope to be at some point in the future. This particular workshop really brought the point home.

I told our workshop participants that when I'd first met with Mike Sebastian in 1987, he worked for a small publishing company called New Clarion Music. He listened to several of my songs and gave me some good suggestions — but no offer of the publishing deal I wanted so badly. I didn't know it then, but, looking back, it's clear that I had many years of practice and hard work ahead of me before my skills would approach the level necessary to compete with the music business pros.

Somehow I managed to survive that rejection and the countless others that stood like mountains keeping me from my dreams. In the fifteen years that separated my meetings with Mike Sebastian I'd worked hard to hone my craft. Looking back, I could see that slowly, almost imperceptibly, those workshops, critiques, rewrites, song camps, networking, and other opportunities I had availed myself of had transformed my songs. I was grateful to be able to provide living proof: sometimes what we wish for is waiting for us, but we may not be ready yet to receive it.

Today, if you've still got more skills to practice, books to read, songs to write, workshops to attend, collaborators to meet, or dreams to dream, remember that it doesn't mean that you can't achieve your goals tomorrow. Well, maybe the day after tomorrow.

REJECTION

"We don't like their sound and guitar music is on its way out," were the words used by an executive at Decca Records in 1962 when he passed on a new group called the Beatles.

There are countless stories about superstars (including Garth Brooks and Whitney Houston) who were rejected time and again, as well as tales of classic songs that met the same fate before being discovered. Stories of multiple artists rejecting songs that later go on to become huge hits are far more common than tales of songs being instantly recognized for their hit potential.

How can we sensitive artists possibly withstand the disappointment, pain, and frustration of the inevitable rejection? The first step is to remind ourselves and accept that rejection is a perfectly normal and expected part of the deal. Then we can begin to find ways to separate our self-worth from our artistic success. This can be a tall order, but the only other option seems to be beating ourselves up—and that's not going to get us to our goals any faster.

Learn from each rejection. Did the listener feel that there were specific problems that recurred in several of your songs (e.g., melodies that were less than memorable or lyric ideas that seemed predictable and uninteresting)? Were your demos praised as being well produced, or were they criticized? Sometimes our songs will be rejected because the person listening is an idiot whose father is a famous producer. From these situations, learn that you need to schedule meetings with other people and that no one individual holds the key to your career. Some rejections remind us that every great song is not right for every artist, or for a particular publisher's needs at a certain time. If you had a face-to-face meeting, let it serve as practice for you to become more comfortable interacting with music business professionals. Each rejection can help teach you that even though it hurts, you can indeed live through the experience and continue to strive toward your goal.

The fact that one particular song may not be very good does not make you a worthless, untalented human being. Nor does the possibility that you might never achieve all of the success you hope for. Unfortunately, the reality is that not everyone who wants to be a professional songwriter or recording artist will be able to earn a living from his or her work. There are simply not enough slots.

Instead of being a superstar recording artist or a hit songwriter, some might channel their love for music into other areas, e.g., becoming a music therapist or high school band leader; working in a music store; working behind the scenes in the music business; or becoming a recording engineer, song publisher, or music teacher. Others might earn their living doing something that's not related to music, while pouring their passion into singing in the church choir, entertaining at homes for the elderly, or performing part-time at weddings or local nightclubs.

Fame and commercial success can be fickle and fleeting. Find joy and fulfillment in the expression of your creativity, instead of in the real and imagined rewards of fame. If you love what you create, as well as the process of creating it, you'll be much happier whether your work ever receives commercial recognition or not. Love what you create and you'll be a success no matter how you pay your bills.

THE TALE OF THE TAIL

People often stare at me as I'm walking away from them. I'd like to think they're admiring my butt. Unfortunately, the much more likely explanation is that they're wondering about the significance of my tail—and I don't mean an appendage extending from the base of my spine.

The tail I'm referring to is made up of my hair. It's like the queue that used to be worn by Chinese men. It's a skinny braid that goes midway down my back. The fact that I look like a conservative middle-aged guy from the front with a braid down his back definitely gets some double takes.

I sometimes joke with people and tell them that it holds the key to my power and that it has deep religious significance. Or that if they tug on the braid it gets me excited. But the truth is that it really does have powerful significance for me.

In 1979, I had a strange dream. At this time in my life I was still working a "day job" and was just beginning to allow myself to imagine pursuing a career as a singer/songwriter. In my dream I saw myself being interviewed on a television talk show. I was a famous recording artist. As the dream unfolded I was asked to play a song on the piano. (Interesting, since I don't play piano.) As I was singing, one of the cameras filmed me from behind and I could see that, in my dream, I had a long braid going down my back. It almost reached my waist.

The next morning, the images from that dream wouldn't leave me. By the end of the day I knew I had to grow the tail that I'd seen in my dream. It seemed to be a symbol, to represent my attaining success—and it would be a lot easier to let a portion of my hair grow than to learn to play the piano!

Throughout the years of struggling I sometimes mused that success was waiting until my tail grew all the way down to my waist, as it had been in my dream. As years went by, there were times when my hairstyle no longer felt consistent with my self-image and I wasn't comfortable drawing attention to myself. I thought about cutting off the tail. Being a rational, logical person, and not very superstitious, I didn't really believe that my hair held the key to my success—did I? Of course not! But a tiny part of me wasn't about to tempt fate by taking any chances.

After ten or twelve years, my tail reached more than halfway down my back, but it didn't seem to be getting any longer. In those years, I'd taken countless workshops and learned more about the craft of songwriting than I'd ever imagined there was to know. My songs were starting to become competitive and I was beginning to earn the attention of publishers. But I was still working miserable "temp" jobs where I tucked my tail, the symbol of my true, creative self, deep inside my shirt and tie. I was making progress, but success was still managing to stay one step ahead of me. My tail had stopped growing—but I hadn't.

Maybe this all sounds crazy. But that dream and the hairstyle it led me to adopt represented my belief that I could, *and would,* someday achieve all the success I'd dreamed of. I needed to believe that, in order to stay on my path in spite of the constant reminders and overwhelming evidence that what I longed for was "impossible." I don't understand why, but on some deep level I always knew that I would become successful. Through the hardest times and deepest disappointments, I held on to that belief like a lifeline.

Each time my father asked me when I was going to give up this "nonsense," go back to school, and get a real job, I didn't have any answers that would make him believe what I knew deep inside my heart. Sometimes my smartass response would be, "You're right. I can't go on like this forever. I'm going to give it a hundred more years and if I haven't become successful, then I'll go back to school!"

I felt a lot more at peace when I realized that it wasn't necessary for my father to share my conviction that I was on the right path. Nor should I have expected him to. I came to accept that I was an adult and had the right to live my life as I had chosen. I no longer needed to convince my father, or anyone else, that I was making the best decisions for me.

Memory is an amazing thing. After I'd had hit songs, my father "always knew" I'd be successful. He was so proud that it was embarrassing. This was a man who carried my resume around and showed it to waitresses and other total strangers. (I'm not kidding.) I could be assured that when we traveled together, anyone within listening distance was sure to know that his son wrote songs for Britney Spears and the Backstreet Boys.

My story had a happy ending, and I'm grateful my father lived long enough to see my success. But what if success had never reached me? Would the years I'd spent at low-paying, miserable jobs, the money I'd invested in demos, and all the sacrifices I'd made have been a terrible mistake? I don't think so. One of the only guarantees life offers is that if we *don't* pursue our dreams, they won't have any chance of coming true. Having that goal gave my life a focus. I made wonderful friends, enjoyed endless hours of studying and honing my craft, and had something to aim for.

PS. I still have that tail. I'm not taking any chances!

SO MUCH ON MY MIND

I'm often asked where my song ideas come from. Well, I was driving to a recent writing session when a really interesting one hit me. Whew! This was a serious relief because I prefer to start with a title or concept and here I was on my way to write with a respected writer/producer and, having done a lot of writing lately, I was fresh out of brilliant, Grammy-worthy ideas. I knew that my cowriter, Robert Ellis Orrall, was preparing to produce a young female country singer on a major label and I wanted a shot at getting a cut on that album. Writing a great song with the producer would certainly give me an edge.

I'd written with Robert only once before, more than ten years ago. As far as I was concerned, the statute of limitations had passed, so it didn't count. Our respective publishers had set up the collaboration. Setting up the right collaborations is one of the most productive actions a publisher can take to forward his or her writers' careers.

Besides wanting to get a cut, I wanted to impress my cowriter and our publishers. But I was exhausted and burnt out following a hectic few weeks, and found myself musing about the excuses I might offer if I was less than brilliant. The truth was that I was preoccupied with getting ready to leave that night for an international business trip that required considerable preparation. My mind was on those things on the ever-growing "to-do" list that I felt compelled to accomplish before boarding the plane. I was busy thinking about the handouts for the workshop, CDs, and other assorted teaching tools I was afraid I'd forget to pack. And did I mention that I was simultaneously trying to work out the details of two recording sessions I'd scheduled for my first day back in town? That meant coordinating singers, studios, cowriters, musicians, and engineers, along with other assorted headaches. The thought occurred to me, "How can I think about writing a song? I've got too much on my mind."

That was it—my great song idea for the young female country artist. "I'm sorry if I seem distracted but I can't concentrate because I've got too much on my mind." And all the things on her mind would be characteristics of this guy that she's crazy about! For example, "I can't seem to think about anything else because my head is filled with thoughts of your lips, your kiss, your touch, your hair, your eyes." That idea arrived just in time because I was about to park my car in front of Peer Music, the publishing company Robert is signed to.

I don't know what to attribute it to, but I've come up with some of my strongest concepts for songs when the pressure was on. Several of those ideas showed up while I was driving en route to my cowriting session. Others whispered in my ear during my morning walk just prior to a writing appointment. Maybe it's the adrenaline rush, or maybe necessity forces me to tune in, making me more open to every potential idea. Whatever the reason, I'm grateful for it.

So, back to the story... I confidently walked into the office and sat down to wait for my cowriter. I got out my cell phone and used the time to call singers, recording studios, and collaborators. I glanced at my watch and noticed that at this point he was fifteen minutes late, which I still consider "on time" on Music Row. When another fifteen minutes had gone by I started to get concerned and called Robert. He said he thought our appointment was scheduled for the following week! (It wasn't, but I learned a valuable lesson—to always confirm my appointments.)

When I got past the initial irritation, I was thrilled because I didn't feel like writing anyway—I literally had too much on my mind. As I packed up my briefcase and headed for the car that song idea wouldn't let go.

Sorry if I seem distracted
I just can't concentrate
There's just too much on my mind (your hair, your lips, your touch, your kiss, your eyes)

When I arrived back at my house, this song demanded to be written—NOW. Packing and getting ready for my trip would have to wait. I filled five pages of my notebook with images that described the things this girl has on her mind. The ones I liked the best eventually became the first four lines of the chorus.

The way you make me laugh when no one can
And how you say we don't need any music to dance
The way your kisses show me you're for real
And how you're not afraid of how I feel

I knew that one of my challenges lyrically with this idea (as with all lyrics) would be to avoid the obvious, predictable lines—which were the first ones that had popped into my head. I thought about how I could tell a story in each verse that would *show*, instead of *telling*, that the singer was obsessed with this guy.

A month elapsed before schedules permitted Robert and me to get back together. In the interim, I had written several melodies to the lyric that our initial writing session had inspired, but I wasn't excited about any of them and decided to bring the idea to Robert. Together, we tweaked the lyric and wrote a melody that we both loved. Somewhere along the way, "Too Much on My Mind" became "So Much on My Mind."

So Much on My Mind

Couldn't find my keys this morning
Got to work an hour late
Sorry if I seem distracted
I just can't concentrate

My brain is overloadin'
And I know the reason why
Emotions overflowin'
I've got so much on my mind

Chorus:
Like the way you make me laugh when no one can
And how you say we don't need any music to dance
The way your kisses show me you're for real
And how you're not afraid of how I feel
And if I forgot to mention
That I've never felt so loved in all my life
Forgive me—I've got so much on my mind

Background Vocal:
Your eyes, your lips, your hugs, your kiss, your style
Your laugh, your touch, your heart, your love, your smile

When I missed my hair appointment
I knew I'd gone off the edge
How can I remember details
When you're fillin' up my head

49

With this preoccupation
It's all you all the time
It's a crazy situation
I've got so much on my mind

(Repeat Chorus)

I can't keep from thinking of
The things that tell me I'm in love

(Repeat Chorus)

Background Vocal Outro:
Your eyes, your lips, your hugs, your kiss, your style
Your laugh, your touch, your heart, your love, your smile
The way you say my name and share my dreams
And how I shiver when you're close to me

©2002
Jason Blume/Robert Ellis Orrall
Zomba Music Inc./Peer Music Publishing

The demo came out great and our publishers are excited about the song. The moral of this story? Look for those ideas that are real for you. If you've got "Too Much on *Your* Mind," I'll bet some of your thoughts are just waiting to become great songs.

Exercise

Make a list of things that are on your mind. For instance:

✓ I need to pay the bills.

✓ I'm lonely and wish I were in a relationship.

✓ I'm worried about my parents; I wish I lived closer to them.

✓ I'm concerned about the future of my marriage.

✓ I'm hurt about last night's argument with my brother.

✓ I can hardly wait until the weekend.

✓ I hate my job and wish I could just write songs.

✓ I've never been so in love.

Choose one or more of the issues you've jotted down and write, in paragraph form, how you feel about it. Don't think about rhyming or being "commercial." Simply express what's on your mind. You can incorporate your ideas into a song later.

AND THE WINNER IS . . .

When I teach workshops, one of the questions I'm frequently asked is, "Is it worthwhile to enter songwriting contests?" It reminds me of one of the worst moments of my life.

In 1989, I was working in the A&R department of RCA Records in Los Angeles. To some people I had the dream job. I had landed this job after being sent out by a temp agency. Now I was getting paid to learn about the music industry from the inside. I was making great connections and interacting with superstar artists. The free albums and backstage passes to concerts were terrific perks. But I was miserable. I wanted to have my own songs on the radio—not be surrounded by other people who were living my dream.

One evening, I came across a tiny ad in the back of a songwriting magazine. It included entry information for the Castlebar Ireland International Song Festival. It sounded like a terrific opportunity to get my songs exposed to an international panel of judges, as well as a chance to win up to $10,000. The only catch was that the deadline to have entries postmarked was the following day—and the entry fee had to be paid with an international bank draft. I didn't know exactly what that was and it sounded like something that would be difficult to obtain. But I was determined.

This was in the days before the advent of CDs, so I made cassette copies of the three songs that I thought were my best shot. I took them with me to work, on the outside chance that I would be able to find one of those international bank drafts. During my lunch break my first stop was the bank across the street, where I was surprised to learn that I had inadvertently found one of the few branches of my bank that could easily issue the required form of payment. The $20-per-song entry fee was steep for me at the time, but I took my chance, ran all the way to the post office, mailed my tape, and managed to get back to work on time—well, almost on time.

Several months went by and I had totally forgotten about the contest when a telegram from Ireland arrived. It was worded very strangely and I honestly couldn't figure out what it was saying. But I guessed it was something good because it began with,

"Congratulations," and ended by requesting that I telephone a number in Ireland ASAP.

The message on the telegram was so confusing that I honestly wasn't excited. It didn't say anything about winning a songwriting competition—but that was indeed what had happened. One of the songs I'd entered, "Wraparound Memory" (written with my friend Bryan Cumming) had won the right to represent the United States in the Castlebar International Song Festival. We would be flown (all expenses paid) to Ireland to perform the song on live television in a competition against the other nine finalists who were each representing their respective nations. It was sort of the "Songwriting Olympics"!

At the time, Bryan was touring as a member of the '50's "Doo-Wop" band, Sha-Na-Na, and commitments made it impossible for him to join me on the trip. So I headed for the Emerald Isle along with my musical director, Wayne Moore. I had never performed on television and had never sung with an orchestra. Knowing that I was not a seasoned performer, I immediately began working with a terrific vocal and performance coach named Lis Lewis. I practiced my song over and over again, incorporating the techniques Lis taught me. Then I practiced some more. I think I practiced even in my sleep. I was a basket case.

I hoped that a relaxing vacation would be just what the doctor ordered to calm my nerves before the competition, and this was my chance to see Ireland. We arrived at Shannon Airport a week prior to the songwriting festival, rented a car, and drove up the rugged west coast of this beautiful country. I'd never seen so many shades of green.

We stayed in quaint little farmhouses and charming old B&Bs along the way. At one point, a cow stuck her head through my bedroom window and "mooed" me awake! As I toured castles, convents, and countryside, my nerves melted away. I became confident. I could sing "Wraparound Memory" inside out and backwards and I knew I would do fine.

Since the TV show would be a live broadcast with an estimated thirty million viewers, there were extensive technical run-throughs. I rehearsed my song with the full orchestra, lights, and cameras at least a half-dozen times—with no glitches. My jitters had been replaced by self-assurance. The judges for the competition were also present at the rehearsals so I told myself that when it was time for the actual show, there would be absolutely no reason to be frightened; I'd have been through the drill plenty of times before. Besides, this was fun—not life and death.

As show time approached, I was amazed at how relaxed and confident I remained. By lottery, I had been assigned the third slot. The sixteen-year-old representing Sweden who was number two had just begun singing her song when a feeling I'd never felt before hit me full force, like a runaway train. There were now approximately three minutes left before it would be time for me to perform my song and the blood in my veins had somehow been replaced with dry ice. Along with my blood went all memory of the words to the second verse of my song.

There were no teleprompters, and with only two-and-a-half minutes left until I would humiliate myself and disgrace the United States in front of thirty million viewers, I frantically searched in vain for a copy of my lyric. Then I realized that my musical director, who was on the opposite side of the stage with the orchestra, had heard this song at least a hundred times and would surely know the lyric.

As the Swedish kid confidently belted out her final chorus I made my way behind the velvet curtains across the stage to the orchestra. My heart was ready to burst out of my chest by the time I reached Wayne. I never knew the meaning of pure horror before that moment as I heard him say, "You wrote the song. How should I know the f%*#g words." This was immediately followed by a booming brogue announcing, "Ladies and Gentlemen, representing the United States of America, please welcome Jason Blume."

I stood out on that stage, buck naked before a firing squad with thirty million witnesses. Well, that's how it felt. As I heard the orchestra play the opening strains of my song, I made a pact with God. If only He'd let words come out of my mouth, I'd be His servant forever. And if the words rhymed and even remotely made sense I'd give up my firstborn and do anything He asked.

I was petrified throughout my first verse. It felt as though my body had turned to stone, and while I was singing all I could do was plaster a phony smile on my face and desperately try to remember that cursed second verse. When it came time for verse two, I still didn't know it and couldn't imagine what would come out of my mouth. I was stunned when the correct words to that second verse tumbled out, just as they had in all of those rehearsals. When the performance from hell was over, I felt as if I'd just been run over by a steamroller. I had the surreal sensation that my time on stage had been just an instant and I could barely remember it. But at least I'd gotten those words right.

To put it mildly, the judges were underwhelmed by my song and by my performance. Needless to say, I did not win the competition. Okay, I'll be honest. I didn't tell this to anyone for many years, but the truth is that I came in last place—and that really hurt. But I'd gotten an incredible, free trip to Ireland and I learned a valuable lesson. From that moment on, I've always kept a copy of my lyrics close at hand whenever I've performed in any high-pressure situation (like a television or radio show). I've never needed to look, but I like having the security blanket.

So, back to the original question: "Is it worthwhile to enter songwriting contests?" My answer is that it depends on what you hope to gain. If you're looking to get "discovered" and become an overnight sensation, it's unlikely that entering a songwriting competition will accomplish this. The large competitions have tens of thousands of entrants, and if your song is good enough to take the grand prize, you probably don't need a contest in order to get noticed.

I have friends who are now professional writers who won lots of money in major competitions before they became successful. But if that's your objective, go in with your eyes open, knowing that the chance of capturing that grand prize may be one hundred thousand to one.

What can you accomplish by entering competitions? If your song receives any acknowledgment (for instance, an "Honorable Mention"), while you might not make any money, you'll have something to add to your resume. When sending a copy of your song to a publisher, it couldn't hurt to attach a sticker on the outside of the envelope stating, "Award-Winning Song Enclosed." Even if you don't win the grand prize, if you're able to place third or fourth in your category, getting a little ego boost is important. We all need an occasional pat on the back to keep trudging down a road that's paved with rejection.

Some competitions (e.g., the New Folk Competition at the Kerrville Folk Festival) can provide important exposure to the winners. Many of the winners (as well as some of the "losers") at Kerrville have gone on to successful careers as performing songwriters. Some of the Christian Music festivals also provide good exposure and networking opportunities.

The bottom line: If you have the money to invest, entering songwriting competitions can be one of many routes to take on the road to success. But don't rely on them to provide your big break.

BUT I'M TOO BUSY

I'm back teaching at Camp SummerSongs in upstate New York. The camp is only a couple of hours from New York City, but, here in the mountains, civilization seems to be a million miles away.

There's no television. There's one public phone being shared by forty people. With a constant line of impatient campers waiting their turn, calls are limited to several minutes. I haven't seen a newspaper in five days. No computer is telling me, "You've got mail." That means I'm not spending any time reading silly jokes, forwarding profound spiritual messages, sharing sentimental stories that teach the meaning of life, seeing how much more money I've lost in the stock market, or checking the latest irresistible travel bargains. I'm teaching two-and-a-half hours a day. That leaves a lot of other hours. When I'm finished teaching, except for mealtimes, I read, write, nap, or go for a walk. That's about it.

It's amazing how creative I can be when I return from a slow walk, having experienced the woods with all my senses. It's incredible how many fresh ideas work their way into my consciousness when I'm not too busy to notice them and take the time to be with them, to explore them, and to write them down. Back home in the real world, it feels like there are a thousand demands on every moment of my time. I never feel this peaceful and centered. I'm too busy trying to be creative and successful.

Of course, a large chunk of time is spent complaining, unwinding, and decompressing from the stress and pressure I put myself under to be creative and successful. So I numb out by watching television or playing solitaire on my computer, chatting on the phone, or responding to e-mails. I wonder how creative and successful I'd be if I stopped trying so hard? What if I unplugged the TV and sold the computer? No chance. But, I think I'll make more time to walk at nearby Radnor Lake, take a nap, read a novel, listen to my heart—and write.

Exercise

According to recent Nielsen Media Research data, by the time the average person reaches age seventy, he or she will have spent the equivalent of seven to ten years watching television. Try an experiment. Choose a day to unplug your television for a twenty-four-hour period. Instead of watching *Wheel of Fortune* (or surfing the web), read a book or go for a walk. Listen to a favorite old album. Or discover a new one. Maybe a long, hot bubble bath would be a treat, or perhaps you might try out a new recipe. Do whatever you feel like doing. Maybe this would be a good night to go out and listen to some live music. On the other hand, you *could* stay at home and make some.

Observe how you use your time away from the television and computer. If you like the results, you might try designating one or two nights each week as "No TV or Computer" nights. You may be surprised at how this affects your creative output — and your sense of serenity.

DO I HAVE TO MOVE?

When I present workshops throughout the U.S., I can always count on certain questions:

- What's Britney Spears really like?
- Can you get me tickets to a Backstreet Boys concert?
- Do I need to move to New York, Nashville, or Los Angeles in order to be successful?

The answers are:

- Sweet, talented, and a hardworking professional.
- No.
- I don't have my crystal ball handy, but some of my thoughts follow.

In response to the question as to whether one has to move or not, I've often heard it said, "If you want to be a movie star, move to Hollywood." The insinuation is that if you want to write country music you move to Nashville; if you want a career in Pop or R&B music you move to L.A. or New York. But it's really not that cut and dried.

Actors typically have to secure an agent and must be available for auditions—sometimes on short notice. Most major television and film projects are based in L.A. or New York, so it's not practical for an actor with aspirations of being a film or TV star to be elsewhere.

For songwriters it's a bit different. We're promoting a product: our songs. In theory it shouldn't matter whether those songs are created in New York City, in a home studio in Kansas, or on a mountaintop in Katmandu. If the songs are great, why should anyone care where you live?

First and foremost, in order to achieve success, your work needs to be exceptional no matter where you live. Few (if any) writers are born with the innate ability to write extraordinary songs. They may have the raw talent but, like a diamond, talent often goes unrecognized unless it's polished and presented to its best advantage.

Songwriting skills typically get honed as a result of attending workshops and classes, receiving constructive feedback and guidance from music industry professionals, and as a result of interacting with other talented, dedicated artists. These are the kinds of opportunities that are primarily available in New York, Nashville, and L.A.—and to a lesser degree (depending on the genre of music) in cities such as Austin, Atlanta, Seattle, Miami, and Minneapolis.

If you cowrite, the odds are good that you'll stand a better chance of finding top-notch collaborators in a major music center that's a mecca for aspiring artists and song-writers than in a remote town. All of these factors add up to the fact that you will probably find more of the networking, educational, and business opportunities that can help you develop your skills and contacts if you're not attempting to do it in a vacuum.

Let's assume that your songs are already exceptional and you don't need any help in the creative department. Can't you just send your songs by mail, MP3, or whatever the latest technology is? Yes. But whom will you send them to? Very few credible publishing companies and record labels accept unsolicited material through the mail. Like so many businesses, this industry is built on personal connections. These connections are made by networking. Obviously, you'll have a better chance of meeting music business profes-sionals and others who might help advance your career if you live in a music center.

A few days ago, I met with an A&R representative at Mercury Records. Yesterday I had a meeting to pitch songs for a platinum-selling artist to her manager. Today, I walked at Radnor Lake, where I ran into one of Nashville's best publishers. Tomorrow I have a meeting at MCA Records. Even if I had the same songs, I wouldn't have these opportu-nities if I still lived in Philadelphia.

When I signed my staff-writing deal with Zomba's Nashville office in 1991, I lived in L.A. However, because my first major recording was by a Country artist, I had far more credibility in Nashville and that's where I was able to secure a deal at a time when I could barely get the time of day from L.A. publishers.

Four times a year I would travel to Nashville and stay for six weeks at a time. These trips were like marathons. I wrote Country songs five days a week. Sometimes I wrote two songs per day. For my Nashville visits, I rented a very inexpensive room in the con-verted attic of a writer's house. I bought an old car for $500 to avoid the expense of car rentals. The arrangement seemed to be working well.

After two years with Zomba, I was making major progress, but there were still no income-producing cuts. My publisher called me into his office for one of *those* talks—the ones that made my stomach curl into knots. This time he said that he believed in my talent and could see the extent of my drive. But my competition was equally talent-ed—and they were giving their careers one hundred percent of their time and energy.

I was spending only four months out of the year in Nashville, essentially one-third of my time. My competition was writing Country songs full time. They were reaping the benefits of a publisher's input twelve months out of the year, as well as having increased opportunities for networking. Some of them had already established connections, a level of credibility, and had written hits. I knew what I needed to do and I began making arrangements to become a full-time resident of Nashville.

It's not feasible for everyone to move. Some people have obligations and responsibilities that would make a move to a music center unadvisable, if not impossible. For others, their career is not enough of a priority to outweigh the substantial emotional costs of pulling up roots and leaving family and friends behind.

If you cannot, or choose not to move, there are still things you can do to maximize your opportunities for advancement. You can make trips to music centers. If your primary focus is writing Country music, a well-timed, weeklong visit to Nashville could include the networking and educational benefits of an intensive three-day NSAI Symposium or Song Camp. It might also include attending one or more workshops, such as the ones I teach each month for BMI (Broadcast Music International) or those presented by SGA (the Songwriters Guild of America). You could also try to schedule an appointment with a representative at one or more of the performing rights organizations (ASCAP, BMI, SESAC), and probably see several awesome live performances. Songwriters who are writing Pop, Rock, or Urban music can achieve comparable results with well-planned trips to New York or L.A.

So, do you "need" to move to Nashville, New York, or L.A.? It's likely that being in the heart of things would improve your odds for success. But there are a lot of factors to consider before taking the plunge. How badly do you want success? How much are you willing to pay to improve your chances, keeping in mind that there are no guarantees? And how much would you be giving up?

The truth is that the overwhelming majority of those hopeful writers who arrive every day will not achieve the success they desire. Therefore, I suggest that you visit the city you're considering moving to. Research real estate, places of worship, recreational activities, cost of living, job opportunities, the weather, and schools if these are important issues to you. Then ask yourself whether you'd be happy living in this city and pursuing your dreams—even if those dreams never come true.

"COMMERCIAL" SONGS

I used to believe that "commercial" was synonymous with selling out, writing bub-blegum fluff. I thought that writing songs with commercial appeal meant sacrificing the integrity of my work to pander to the lowest common denominator. Now I have a very different opinion.

"Commercial" simply means what sells—and that includes Creed, Dido, Bjork, Sheryl Crow, Eminem, Ja Rule, U2, Alicia Keys, and Sarah McLachlan, as well as 'N Sync and Britney Spears. I've stopped confusing *commercial* with trite, contrived fluff. Sometimes they're one and the same, but they don't have to be.

I'm finding I can definitely sell, without selling out. I have songs that emanated purely from my heart and still wound up on albums that sold millions of copies. The song "She's Gonna Fly" (a.k.a. "On Angel's Wings," cowritten with Karen Taylor-Good) on Collin Raye's album *Tracks*, on my own CD, *The Way I Heard It*, as well as on Karen's *On Angel's Wings* was written solely to express what was in my and my cowriter's hearts. While the lyric is not literally a true story, it was based on a very real situation. It deals with issues including Alzheimer's and aging. For my cowriter and me, every word, note, and breath of that song is connected to genuine emotion, and we've got the empty Kleenex boxes to prove it. "She's Gonna Fly" was probably a successful song *because* it expressed powerful, intense emotions, not because it avoided them.

After twenty years, I've learned my craft well enough to also write for specific proj-ects that are not necessarily "real" for me. I'm not a twelve-year-old girl, but I've acquired the skills that allowed me to imagine what Britney's fans might want to sing or hear. Is it "selling out" to write a song that millions of young, impressionable fans can embrace? Is it selling out if you give preteens the words and music to help them express what they're feeling inside? It is—*if* you're doing it strictly to try and pull the proverbial wool over the listeners' eyes (and ears) by cranking out music you don't care about in order to make money. That probably won't work, anyway.

For me, writing songs like Britney's "Dear Diary," which was born of pure imagina-tion, as opposed to personal experience, is a very rewarding experience—and not just financially. I remember when that idea popped into my head. I was sitting at my computer when I suddenly thought it would be a novel, fresh approach to write a song in which the singer is talking directly to, confiding in, and even asking advice of, her diary. Later that evening I half-jokingly mentioned to a friend, "I'm about to get another Britney Spears cut," because I was so certain this idea was perfect for her very young female listeners. I had a cowriting session scheduled a few days later with Eugene Wilde, another Zomba writer who'd enjoyed wonderful success with the Backstreet Boys. I brought Eugene the idea and we cowrote the music very easily.

Initially, one of the decision makers at the record label feared the lyric was too young for Britney, and was concerned about the ending of the song being too sad. I rewrote the lyric and presented them with four different endings to choose from while I crossed my fingers and held my breath.

When the label executive asked if we would be willing to sit down with Britney and incorporate her ideas for the ending of "Dear Diary" into the lyric I was ecstatic, but I suspected it would be a nightmare working with her. I expected a snotty, arrogant diva with "attitude." I was wrong. Britney was a pleasure to work with: professional, funny, respectful, and very much a "regular" nice teenager. Her ideas for the song were terrific and she worked hard to sing the demo just the way I imagined it.

This incredible day ended with Britney posing for pictures and signing a stack of autographs for nieces, nephews, and assorted friends—just before Justin Timberlake arrived at the studio to pick her up. The *Oops, I Did It Again* album that "Dear Diary" was included on has sold more than 16 million copies worldwide.

I enjoy being a storyteller and working in various genres that are not all autobiographical. Sometimes it's as satisfying for me to write a song that makes the listeners smile or want to dance as it is to bare my soul. If writing for artists other than you feels like selling out, don't do it. No one has a gun to your head forcing you to be a songwriter, or any specific kind of songwriter.

For me, there's room for both kinds of writing. What makes a song commercially viable is its potential to connect to millions of listeners. The key is taking an idea that's born in your heart and expressing it in a fresh way (melodically and lyrically) that can touch millions of people you've never met. This typically is accomplished by using tried-and-true methods, tools, and techniques:

- Learning effective song structures.
- Discerning the difference between writing for yourself and writing for a mass audience.
- Identifying ideas that will speak to your audience.
- Crafting lyrics that express your ideas in ways that allow your listeners to

clearly feel what you intend them to feel. (There are tools and techniques to help you accomplish this—without compromising the emotion that initially propelled you to write the song.)*

- Composing melodies that are consciously crafted to be memorable, accessible, easy to sing, and melodic—and not just there to accommodate the words.

Incorporate these tools into your songs and you'll see that you can indeed be commercial. And real.

Exercise

If your goal is to have your songs on the radio, listen to the current hits on the radio. Find those artists who don't write their own songs, yet record songs that you love. Study and analyze those songs. Examine the tools and techniques the writers used lyrically, as well as melodically, by answering the following questions:

✓ Do the lyrics sound natural and conversational? Or are they flowery and poetic?

✓ How many syllables are contained in each line of each of the verses? How many in the choruses?

✓ What structure did the writers use (e.g., Verse-Chorus-Verse-Chorus-Bridge-Chorus)?

✓ Does the lyric tell a clear story? Or is it filled with symbolism and non-literal imagery?

✓ Does the melody incorporate repetition? If so, where?

✓ Is the chorus melody higher or lower in range than the verses?

✓ Are there different rhythms in the various sections of the song?

✓ Is some aspect of the idea unique?

✓ Is the concept something that you would expect millions of listeners to relate to?

Now write your own song by using the tools and techniques that have proved to be successful.

---

*An in-depth examination of lyric techniques and tools can be found in Step II, "Writing Effective Lyrics," in 6 *Steps to Songwriting Success*, and the instructional CD, *Writing Hit Lyrics with Jason Blume* (Moondream Music).

PICTURE THE VIDEO

Once, while writing with a collaborator, I noticed he was doodling and drawing little stick figures all over his lyrics. When my curiosity got the better of me I asked what he was doing. He replied, "My publisher asked me to include more pictures in my lyrics."

One of the basic tools of effective lyric writing is "show—don't tell," meaning craft your lyrics with words that include images, actions, colors, and details to enable your listener to *visualize* the action. This allows your audience to enter the song and be a part of it, instead of on the outside looking in. It helps your listener to feel what you feel, instead of just knowing what you know—and one of your lyric's primary jobs is to evoke emotion.

Crafting lyrics that tell stories and use detailed, descriptive words is one of the hardest things for me to do as a songwriter. It would be an understatement to say that it does not come naturally. It's much easier for me to cut to the chase and tell the listener what I want them to feel or what it is that I feel. Unfortunately, these are not very effective ways to evoke empathy.

I've heard it said that there's no better way to learn than to teach, and I know that's true. When I wrote the chapters and the exercises in 6 *Steps to Songwriting Success: The Comprehensive Guide to Writing and Marketing Hit Songs* that teach the reader how to tell a story with imagery and detail, I was forced to create examples of the ways that we, as writers, can express abstract emotions (i.e., loneliness, being in love, being happy) by using detailed, concrete images. It felt strange to be teaching others to do what I felt I did so poorly. But I found that when my back was against the wall and I pushed myself, I *could* generate those visually oriented images that play such an important role in effective lyric writing. I learned that even though it wasn't easy, and it wasn't always fun, with practice and persistence I could incorporate this important tool into my writing.

One of the techniques that helped me was imagining the hypothetical video for my song. If I couldn't "see" something on the video that played in my mind, I didn't include it in my lyric. Since a viewer can't see what a person is feeling, I avoided phrases like:

- "He's as sad as can be."

- "She feels like she can fly."
- "I'm the happiest man on earth."

For instance, instead of expressing "she's lonely" by simply telling the listener:

- "She's so lonely without him."
- "She feels so blue deep inside."
- "Loneliness is all she feels."
- "Her heart is breaking with loneliness."

I learned to *show* what "she's lonely" looks like:

- "She stays up all night crying in that big old empty bed."
- "She plays solitaire every Saturday night."
- "She sips her wine at a table for one."
- "She sits alone in the dark watching that same sad old movie on TV."

The kind of writing I'm describing is the mainstay of great country lyrics; it's also the heart of rap. However, incorporating detailed, original imagery and telling a story, instead of stating what the singer feels, can be a powerful tool in *all* styles of music. If our songs are to rise above the competition, we have to find ways to set them apart, both melodically and lyrically. Acquiring and using this tool can help make your lyrics unique and give your listeners a reason to choose your songs over those written by the competition.

The lesson? I learned that just because it doesn't come naturally or easily, doesn't mean I can't acquire a skill.

Exercise

What are those songwriting skills that your head tells you that you can't acquire? Do you think you can't write a catchy melody or a lyric that tells a story and incorporates detailed, fresh imagery? Do you have a voice in your head that says you'll never be able to craft a particular type of song (perhaps an Alternative Rock song, a Holiday song, or one that would rise to the top of the Pop charts)? Do the following:

- ✓ List those skills that you'd like to acquire.
- ✓ Set aside thirty minutes this week to practice one of them.
- ✓ Next week choose a different skill from your list and work on that one.

Don't expect perfection the first time you try a new technique. With practice and persistence you'll be amazed to learn how many things you can do that you were so sure were "impossible."

D-DAY

Today is one of those days I truly dread. My stomach's in knots and I barely slept last night. Every couple of months I demo a batch of five of my Country songs "Nashville style"—and today's the day.

The experience of recording a five-song Nashville demo with a live band is very different from recording a Pop or R&B/Urban demo. For me, recording Pop and R&B is much less stressful; the musical tracks for these demos are typically "programmed" by a keyboard player, one song at a time. The bass, drum sounds, and all keyboard parts are typically played on the keyboard by the programmer. In many instances the programmer can also approximate the sound of guitars. But if needed, live guitars can be added when the programmer has finished all the other parts. When recording a Pop or R&B demo, since you are typically working with only one musician/programmer, if your budget permits, you can take as much time as you need to try out various parts, experiment with different arrangements and sounds, and then go back and change things later. Not so with Country.

In preparation for today's demo session, I've spent weeks putting my songs under a microscope, getting my publisher's critiques, rewriting (and rewriting and rewriting...), booking a studio, hiring a recording engineer, securing and confirming musicians, and selecting the best vocalists for each song. I've also gotten several professional opinions and narrowed down the list of songs, selecting those that I think stand the best shot of being recorded by a major artist.

After I'd chosen which songs to demo, then came the joy of typing lyrics and mailing work tapes to all the singers before the session so they could let me know what key would be best for them. Scheduling the order of the songs so that all of my collaborators can attend the session was like piecing together a jigsaw puzzle. I made a compilation CD of work tapes of the songs we'll be recording so they'll all be in one place when I need to play them for the musicians at the session. I've also printed multiple copies of the lyric sheets.

The past week has been spent listening to my rough work tapes over and over again and obsessing about song arrangements—which instruments will sound best on each song (should I use a piano or a B-3 organ sound, or both); how long should the instrumental solo be; what musical phrase would make the most attention-grabbing intro? I've looked over each line of lyric and melody and made last-minute adjustments. Then I adjusted my adjustments. Yesterday, I sat with one of the musicians and oversaw the writing of the chord charts. Preparing for this demo recording session has been practically a full-time job for the past week.

One of the reasons that I've been so attentive to every minute detail is to cover the fact that I'm terrified. Terrified that my songs aren't good enough; that I won't be able to express what I want to the musicians; that the demos will sound horrible. Bear in mind that I've been doing this for more than twelve years. It always makes me this anxious—and the sessions typically go well.

But some of my fears are based on reality. I'm not fluent in "musician." Nashville uses a number-based chord system that I've learned to understand (barely), but I don't think that way automatically. Once the recording session begins, it feels as though the time goes by in an instant. Next thing I know I've spent thousands of dollars and the demos that will play such an important role in my future success are carved in stone. No wonder I get nervous.

Here's how a typical professional Nashville demo session goes down. The musicians are hired for a three-hour block—either 10:00 a.m. to 1:00 p.m.; 2:00 p.m. to 5:00 p.m.; or 6:00 p.m. to 9:00 p.m. The band will include electric guitar, acoustic guitar, bass, drums, and keyboards. Depending on the budget and what you're envisioning for your songs, you might also include either a musician who can "double" on fiddle, banjo, and/or mandolin, or one who plays pedal steel guitar, lap steel, and dobro.

By the time the recording engineer places the microphones correctly and adjusts his equipment to record each instrument to its best advantage, twenty minutes or more may have elapsed. (During this time, I'm nervously checking my watch, trying my best to make nonchalant chitchat with the musicians and controlling the urge to scream, "We're wasting precious time. Let's get started!") When the sound levels are set, the musicians gather together and listen to the rough work tape of the first song. They follow along with the chord chart that has been prepared in advance.

After listening to the rough version of the song one time through they get to work. The chord charts do not tell them exactly what notes to play. Their job is not just to play the chords correctly and in time, but to create the "radio-friendly" licks that will help get the songs recorded. These guys are unsung heroes and their contributions are enormous. It really can make the difference between success and "almost." That's why I hire the best musicians available.

The top demo players in Nashville regularly play on "master" sessions (albums), but are willing to play on demos on those days when they're not working on major album projects. The musicians I hire are union members and the list of albums they've played on sounds like a Who's Who of popular music—Faith Hill, Lonestar, Billy Joel, Garth Brooks, the Eagles, Reba McEntire, Linda Ronstadt, James Taylor, Amy Grant, George Harrison, Trisha Yearwood, and more. FYI, master sessions pay at a much higher rate than demos and can contribute important credits to a musician's resume. Therefore, if one of your "players" gets an opportunity to work on a master session (even at the last minute), it's understood that he or she will bow out and help you to find an equally talented replacement.

The musicians typically run through the song two or three times before locking in on the final version. As I listen, I scribble notes on the chord chart and then let them know what's working for me as well as which parts I'd like them to change. But bear in mind that I'm not very technically oriented. My comments might be along the lines of: "Would you try it just a bit slower?"; "I'm looking for something a little quirkier on the intro."; "Can you make it sound more like traditional Country?"; "I'd like the guitar solo to be a bit more melodic."; or "What can we do to give it more of a Bluegrass feel?"

The Nashville "number system" expresses chords as numbers. For example, in the key of "C," "C" is "one," "D" is "two," "E" is "three," etc. This allows the musicians to change keys effortlessly without the necessity of rewriting the charts. There are many other symbols that are used, including "diamonds," "pluses," and "minuses." It's like speaking a different language and might sound like, "After the split-one over five be sure to diamond the forty-four eleven."

To me, a Nashville chart looks like a cross between an algebra equation and hieroglyphics. I couldn't tell the difference between a forty-four eleven and a fifty-five twelve if my life depended on it. But I do know what sounds good to me and what doesn't sound like I intended. Instead of allowing myself to become intimidated, I remind myself that my expertise is as a songwriter, not as a musician. I don't have to be able to understand the technical stuff. Nor do I have to be ashamed because I don't. But I do have to be able to find a way to express what my vision is for my song in such a way that the final demo sounds the way I'd imagined—or even better.

For me, the answer is to find a "translator"; someone who can understand what I want and help me convey that to the musicians. I've had great success working with Herb Tassin, an excellent recording engineer/producer who does just that for me. If you don't speak "musician" fluently, you need to find an ally: someone in the band, or an engineer who can do this for you.

It's incredible, but in twenty to thirty minutes the music for each song is one hundred percent finished. This process is then repeated for the next song, and the next. At the end of the three-hour recording session, I typically have recorded the music for five songs. Depending on the complexity of these songs, I might even squeeze in a sixth song, or have to settle for just four.

The pressure is intense because time is money. If I record six songs during the three-hour session, my cost per song averages less than $500. But if I only manage to record four songs, I may be looking at $700 or more per song. Of course, if I've cowritten the songs, these costs are shared by my collaborators—presuming they have agreed to record the demo.

Later this evening or on another day, I'll return to the studio and record vocals with the session singers whom I think will be best suited for each of the songs. I'm a good singer. I've recorded my own album and I've sung on radio and television. But in order to serve my songs the best, I've learned to put my own ego aside and hire the singer who is most appropriate for each song. If I'm completely honest with myself, that's typically not me.

Nashville is overflowing with awesome vocalists who are willing to sing demos. Many of them will be stars in their own right at some point in the future. These singers are available very inexpensively—typically around $100 to $150 per song (at the time of this book's publication), including all background vocals. Pop vocals usually cost more because they typically require additional background vocals. Among those singers who have sung demos prior to becoming successful recording artists are Country music stars Trisha Yearwood, Joe Diffie, Garth Brooks, Alan Jackson, Faith Hill, and many more. I've even critiqued a demo that had been sung by a talented fifteen-year-old before she hit the top of the pop charts as Pink. I want the very best chance for my songs and I know that I'm not in these singers' league as a vocalist.

The last step in the recording process is the mix; that will be done tomorrow. Mixing is one of the many aspects of the demo-recording process about which I have the barest minimum of expertise. It's where the engineer will balance the levels of each individual instrument and vocal, and adjust the treble, bass, reverb, delay, compressors, and lots of other little knobs and machines that I know very little about, in order to make all the individual parts come together to sound like a hit—hopefully. The best thing I can do is to hire a recording engineer whom I trust and let him do what he does best. My input is limited to comments like, "I think I need the vocal to be a little bit louder on that third line," or "Can I hear it with a tad less electric guitar on the solo?"

I've written the best songs I'm capable of. I've done all I could do to prepare for this session. I went for a walk this morning and listened to the songs over and over again on that radio in my mind. I've reminded myself that, luckily, I don't need to be an expert in every area of the demo process; I just need to work with people who are. Now, I'm writing a chapter in this book to help diffuse the fear. The only thing left to do is to go have a great demo session.

Like every aspect of successful songwriting, learning to produce professional-sounding demos is a skill that improves with practice. It's not realistic to expect the first songs we ever write to be the best work of our career. Nor should we count on our initial attempts at recording demos to be perfect.

If all of this information seems totally overwhelming, don't despair. There are excellent, reasonably priced demo services that do all the work for you by mail. You simply send in a rough work tape along with a description of how you hope the demo will sound. The demo service does the rest. Since many of these services are located in major music centers, they have access to top musicians and vocalists.

Of course, if you're not at the session, it's unlikely that even the best demo service will be able to capture every nuance that you might imagine for your song. They're not mind readers. But using a reliable demo service is a viable option for those writers who either lack the ability or the inclination to produce their own demos. You can find these services by seeking referrals from other songwriters, reading magazines that are geared to songwriters, and searching the Internet. Most of them will be glad to send you a sample of their work, as well as a price list.

Postscript: It's the next day. I survived another demo session. I've got five new demos and they sound great! Now comes the hard part—getting them recorded.

FINDING GREAT IDEAS

When I moved to Nashville almost ten years ago, Pat Alger was one of those writers I was in awe of. I remember seeing him at a party and being too intimidated even to say "hello." Tomorrow I have a cowriting session with him.

I'm nervous, excited, and terrified at the prospect of writing with Pat. I've run into him at music industry events and in the supermarket and he seems like a nice, regular guy, but I can't seem to forget that he wrote some of the songs that moved me most. As far as I'm concerned, "Unanswered Prayers" and "The Thunder Rolls" (both recorded by Garth Brooks) are masterpieces. While they're not as well known, Kathy Mattea's "Seeds" and Hal Ketchum's "Small Town Saturday Night" are among my all-time favorite songs. Pat cowrote all of these.

Once again, my biggest fear is that I won't come up with anything brilliant to bring to the table. I've known our appointment was approaching for the past month, but I haven't thought of any truly profound, original lyric ideas, or even one melody that feels like a hit waiting to happen, in that time. So, in desperation, I decided to look through an old file folder that's overflowing with scraps of paper containing lyric ideas that were scribbled in dark movie theaters, at concerts, at stoplights, in restaurants, and everywhere else in between.

The Boy Scouts' motto "Be Prepared" comes to mind. I always suggest that writers come into cowrites primed with several strong lyric ideas, melodic snippets, or both, depending on their particular strengths. As I mentioned earlier, I call these "song starts." Coming into a collaboration session with the beginning of a good lyric or melodic idea takes some of the pressure off and reduces the chance of it being unproductive—especially if you happen to wake up feeling like a brain-dead slug on that particular day.

Before my writing appointments I try to come up with new ideas and go through those napkins, envelopes, receipts, ticket stubs, and other scraps of paper that I've scrawled titles or phrases onto. (I've heard it said facetiously that you can't find a napkin in Nashville, implying that all of them have been used by songwriters to write down their ideas!) Periodically I also dig out the old cassettes that I've shoved in the back of my desk drawer, and the ones that are strewn all over the floor. You know the ones I mean—those tapes you sang those cool melodies into and intended to label, but never quite got around to it.

In preparation for my writing session with Pat Alger, I looked at hundreds of potential song titles and lyric phrases that I'd jotted down over the past ten years. At least a hundred of those "starts" have grown up to become full-fledged songs. I noticed that the majority of my old ideas shared some common traits. Most of them contained clever, cutesy twists on words (e.g., "I Want the *Good* Life and I Want it *Bad*"), or they were based on altering a common phrase (e.g., "Faster than the Speed of Love"). Others were based on the way some words sounded when I put them together (e.g., "The Tupelo Two-Step"; "Honk if You Love to Honky-Tonk"). The vast majority of my titles and ideas shared one common bond: instead of being born in my heart, they'd been manufactured in an attempt to come up with a "hit" song—and that seemed painfully obvious to me ten years later. There wasn't a shred of genuine emotion attached.

I wasn't writing these songs because I had something I needed or wanted to share through my words and music. I was writing because I wanted to be a successful, rich, famous songwriter. There's nothing wrong with being a successful, rich, famous song-writer. It's just that it's more likely to happen if I'm writing because I love writing songs—not because I love cashing royalty checks.

There was another common denominator in many of those song ideas. The titles that weren't clever or cutesy tended to be pretty mundane and unimaginative. On a big blackboard in my publisher's office there's a listing of songs the company publishes that have recently been recorded by major artists. I looked at that board today and noticed that most of the songs indeed had titles that were unusual, intriguing, or in some way attention-grabbing. Those titles included "She's Gonna Fly," "That's Just Jesse," "There Is No Arizona," "Shiver," "I'm Already There," "I Should Be Sleeping," "Wings," and "Dear Diary."

In looking through my old song ideas I saw that a disproportionately large percentage of my titles seemed to contain the words "heart" or "love." There's nothing wrong with using these words, and, of course, there are lots of terrific songs that used "heart" or "love" in the title, or prominently within the lyric. Some examples include "Unbreak My Heart," "From the Bottom of My Broken Heart," "What's Love Got to Do with It," "Love Is a Four-Letter Word," and "Love in an Elevator." However, the writers of these songs found unique angles. That's one of our most important jobs as lyricists. My song ideas and titles weren't nearly as imaginative.

If you were screening hundreds of songs five days a week, which of the following titles would be more apt to grab your attention?

- "I Really Love You"
- "With All My Heart"
- "I'll Give You My Love"

or

- "I Hope You Dance"
- "It's Hot in Heere"
- "It Wasn't Me"

When I went into my office this morning I made a point of counting how many of the recently recorded songs on my publisher's blackboard had titles with "heart" or "love" in them. Out of forty-two song titles listed on the board, there were only two that included these words. Please note that I'm not suggesting that you never write a song unless it has a scintillating title. Dolly Parton reached Number One *three times* as the writer of "I Will Always Love You."

I'm not saying that you should never use "heart" or "love" in your titles. I've had success on several occasions with songs that included one of these words in the title (e.g., "I'll Never Stop Loving You," recorded by Britney Spears; "Back to Your Heart," recorded by the Backstreet Boys; "I Had a Heart, recorded by Darlene Austin; and "Heart," recorded by Collin Raye). But in each instance I tried to find an interesting, new approach. In the chorus of "I Had a Heart," my cowriter Bryan Cumming and I wrote:

I had a heart
You turned it to stone
When it needed love
You left it alone
I had a heart
But you made it break
Now where I had a heart
There's just a heartache

There are no "rules" in songwriting. But using unique, fresh titles and concepts will give your songs an edge in a very competitive arena.

My old song ideas were a part of my journey, but none of them became hits. With the clarity that often comes only in retrospect I can see that those ideas were empty and contrived. Those kinds of songs are rarely successful, because it's tough to fool millions of listeners. If you're trying to write about something you don't feel connected to, the problem is that somewhere across town another writer who really does feel it is probably writing about a similar idea.

Every song doesn't have to be deep and cathartic. There's lots of room for fun, uptempo songs that make people want to dance or just smile. But write them because it's what you feel, not because you heard that publishers want uptempo songs with positive messages. If you write a piece of "fluff," do it because you're feeling "fluffy." The real deal is hard to beat.

It's a lot tougher to write from your heart, but well worth it. If your song never becomes a hit on the radio (and most of them won't), at least you'll have written something that you're proud of. Write songs with artistic integrity that mean something to you and will touch listeners, and you will feel good about your work, even if the only ones who hear it are your friends and relatives.

Postscript: The writing session with Pat was a pleasant experience. I learned that in addition to being a terrific talent, he's a super-nice guy and he makes a killer salad. But alas, that indefinable chemistry didn't show up that day and we wrote a song that was only "good." I was disappointed, but the world did not come to an end.

Exercise

Write a song that expresses an emotion or emotions you've never dared to write about before. Be vulnerable. Be real. This is an exercise in accessing and expressing your feelings. Through your words and music share the deepest part of you that you've kept locked away until now. When you've finished this song, no one ever has to hear it if you don't want them to.

HEY, MON

I had decided to cut back on my teaching in order to devote more time to my own writing. I instructed my assistant Neil Rice, who books all of my speaking engagements, to say, "No" to any requests for the upcoming year. Then the offer came in to teach in Jamaica . . . and I started packing.

Well, actually, before accepting the job, I expressed my concern that I might not be the best teacher for the job. My knowledge of Jamaican music begins and ends with a few Bob Marley hits. I didn't know how Reggae songs differed from the Pop, Country, and R&B/Urban songs I was familiar with. Did they use different structures? Choruses? Verses? Bridges? I knew that I probably couldn't tell the difference between a "good" and a "great" Reggae song and therefore, regrettably, was probably not the right instructor for the job.

But the woman who had contacted me from Jamaica was very persuasive and she was convinced that I was the person she wanted to teach Jamaican songwriters how to write for the U.S. and international markets. She insisted that "music is music," and that those elements that make listeners love a song would transcend cultures. I believe that's true, but I was still hesitant because I knew that some of the tools and techniques would differ. I agreed to take on the job only when I was assured that I would have the help of Mikey Bennett, an esteemed Jamaican writer and producer who would be available throughout my presentation to explain how the concepts I taught fit and did not fit with the Jamaican market.

It would be an understatement to say that the trip did not get off to a good start. On the little form that I had to present to customs I had checked the box that said I was entering the country for business. When the immigration officer asked to see my work visa, I knew I was in big trouble. No one had ever mentioned a work visa and, needless to say, the only Visa I had was the one that had been issued by Citibank. Thirty minutes, two Gestapo agents, and some serious quick thinking later, I was shaking but permitted to enter the country.

I was pretty upset from the immigration ordeal and figured I'd better make a pit stop before leaving the airport. About ten yards away from the immigration office there were two rooms, side by side, that both seemed to be identically marked "Wash Room." I looked at both of the doors but couldn't discern any difference between the two. I peeked into one of the rooms and saw that it contained private stalls. So in my traumatized state, I figured, "I'm in a foreign country," and although it felt a bit odd I assumed men and women must use the same washrooms in Jamaica.

It was a truly bizarre feeling to look down and see high-heeled shoes in the stall next to mine. As I was washing my hands the woman attached to the high heels emerged from the stall, took one look at me and began screaming. Since I don't normally have that effect on people I figured out that I was in the ladies' room. I ran out muttering my apologies before the police arrived.

I figured things had to get better. After settling in and taking a brief rest at my hotel in Kingston, I met the workshop's sponsors for dinner at an outdoor café. The food and conversation were excellent. I was informed that my workshop, "Songwriters' Bootcamp," was sponsored by JAMPRO, a division of the Jamaican government's Department of Economic Development. It was intended as an opportunity to stimulate economic growth by teaching Jamaican writers to write for the U.S. and global markets. No one had mentioned this little detail to me before.

When I realized that the government's hope was that the participants would make lots of money as songwriters to boost the Jamaican economy, I almost choked on my jerk chicken. My initial thought was, "Teach them to be accountants, computer operators, dental hygienists, truck drivers, teachers, lifeguards, pastry chefs, insurance salesmen, massage therapists, trapeze artists—*anything* but songwriters if your primary goal is for them to make money."

I gently explained how incredibly difficult it is for even the most talented songwriters to earn a living from their craft. In between the mouth-watering pumpkin soup and the to-die-for fried plantains, I mentioned that I'd struggled for more than eleven years before beginning to support myself (albeit, barely above poverty level) as a songwriter. I explained that it was an additional five years, for a total of more than sixteen years of sacrifice and living hand to mouth, before I got the lucky break that lead to my earning some serious money. I made it clear that songwriting, like most creative endeavors, comes with no guarantee of financial reward.

Our retreat would be held high in the Blue Mountains at the Jamaica Defence Force's training facility (so *that's* why it was called "Songwriter's Boot Camp"). The first day of classes went great. The weather was perfect and I taught outdoors facing a view of mountain peaks that took my breath away. There were moments when I could look down and watch the clouds rolling by below us.

As I taught those common denominators that seem to consistently be found in successful songs, it seemed obvious that these same elements would indeed transcend different styles of music. Regardless of the genre, a lyric needs to be something that listeners can relate to, something a singer would want to say and an audience would want to hear. When I taught that in order to rise above the competition we need to write melodies and lyrics that are special, original, and fresh—not just "good," but "exceptional"—I knew that what I was teaching applied across the board to all types of music.

I explained that whether we're writing Pop, Country, R&B, Reggae, or any other style of music, we have to give artists, producers, and record label executives compelling reasons to choose *our* songs instead of the ones written by other writers (including the artist and producer). The participants hung on my every word and asked lots of questions, so I figured I must be connecting with them.

As the workshop progressed, I listened to the participants' songs and made suggestions that I thought would help. They thought I was absolutely brilliant each time I came up with a clever twist on words or an interesting way to approach a title. I assured them that when I arrived in Nashville I thought the writers and publishers on Music Row must be geniuses and worried that I would never be able to master the art of lyric writing the way it seemed those professionals had.

I explained that the Nashville professionals didn't necessarily have more natural talent than I had, but they had acquired and practiced specific skills that are learnable. The successful Nashville writers had trained themselves to look for those clever twists on words and opposites (e.g., "You Hurt Me *Bad* in a Real *Good* Way," "You Really Had Me *Goin'*, but Now I'm *Gone*") and to write by telling stories filled with imagery, detail, color, and action. These are skills that I've been able to develop with conscious effort, practice, and perseverance.*

Time for lunch! I like to be adventurous when I travel and prefer to eat what the locals eat. But lunch was a little too adventurous for my palate. The cuttlefish was loaded with bones and was so salty it made me want to gag. I picked at it to be polite and figured I'd be safe with the boiled green bananas and callaloo greens—but everything had been boiled in with the salted fish. It all tasted alike, and I couldn't get it down. I was an hour's drive from civilization, so lunch was fresh fruit and bread.

By the end of the day, I was relieved to be learning that the tools and techniques I teach did indeed have relevance to these writers. A twilight concert under the stars was heralded by hundreds of bats swirling around us. An occasional cow wandered by as we

---

*For exercises to practice looking for opposites and clever twists on words see 6 *Steps to Songwriting Success: The Comprehensive Guide to Writing and Marketing Hit Songs*, Chapter 3.

listened to some terrific raw talent presented stripped down to melodies and lyrics sung *a capella* or with an acoustic guitar. It was magical and I went to bed filled with gratitude for this opportunity.

We woke the next morning at 6:00 a.m. to start the day with a hike. The views that greeted us were truly spectacular and the weather clear and chilly—probably at least thirty degrees cooler than the sweltering temperatures in the city, an hour and 7,500 feet below us. We returned invigorated and relaxed from our walk, and ready to study melody techniques, but were greeted by the news that a hurricane was headed directly for us and that we needed to evacuate the premises in the next forty minutes! An hour later we'd been loaded into army transport trucks and were headed back down the mountain to Kingston.

The workshop continued on safer ground in the city. Day Two focused on melody techniques. I was intrigued by the fact that several of the students could not seem to grasp the difference between the definitions of "melody" and "rhythm." As we discussed it, I realized that rhythm is such an integral part of their music that it was hard for them to differentiate it from melody. By the end of a very satisfying second day we had discussed the importance of incorporating repetition into our melodies, using rhythms that were fresh and original, prosody, using logical sequences, varying the rhythms between sections, signature licks, and much more. I could see the light bulbs going on over their heads.

Unfortunately, our uninvited guest, Hurricane Iris, was rapidly approaching and the decision was made to end the workshop a day earlier than anticipated. I crammed in as much material as I possibly could. Drawing on what was all around us, I concluded the workshop by talking about the use of "storm" imagery to convey the impending end of a relationship and left them with an assignment to write a song about the fact that a storm was on its way.

After sharing lots of hugs with my talented new friends, I returned to my hotel to wait for my first hurricane. Flights in and out of the country were canceled. The howling wind and torrential rain had knocked out television reception and made leaving the hotel a really bad idea. So there I was, stuck all alone in a hotel room in Jamaica. I did what any songwriter would do under the circumstances—I wrote a Reggae song. Luckily, the path of the hurricane swerved and Kingston avoided a direct hit.

So, I had quite an adventure in Jamaica, although it wasn't exactly the experience I'd had in mind. I learned that those elements that allow music to enter listeners' hearts really do transcend cultures and musical genres. I was also exposed to some wonderful artists and gained respect for Reggae music and for the warm, wonderful people who write it and listen to it. I hope my Jamaican students learned as much as I did.

Exercise

Take a moment to observe your immediate surroundings. Jot down your observations by answering the following questions:

✓ What's the weather?

✓ What do you see?

✓ What do you smell?

✓ Who are you with?

For instance: It's hot; there are mosquitoes; there's not a cloud in the sky; I'm sitting under a magnolia tree; I can smell chicken on the grill; my cousin is visiting.

Now begin a song based on the images you've listed. For example (using the images shown above):

It's ninety-three degrees—The mosquitoes are buzzin'
Went on a picnic with my favorite cousin
Barbecue chicken and apple pie
Sweet magnolia under clear blue sky

Incorporating action and using literal, physical descriptions in your lyrics lets you tell a story and allows your listeners to "witness" the scene unfolding. It's a terrific tool to help avoid the common pitfall of telling how you feel instead of telling a story. This allows your listeners to feel what you feel.

IF YOU WANT TO BE
ON THE RADIO

One of the biggest challenges I've faced as a songwriting instructor has been explaining to some of my older students why their melodies and lyrics sound old-fashioned. It's not an issue of whether their songs are "good" or "bad," but whether they are appropriate for current radio. Everything we write doesn't have to be "radio friendly," but if your goal is to write a hit, your songs better not sound as if they've been lost in a time warp.

Thanks to my clarinet teacher, I grew up listening to and loving the Big Bands that reached their peak popularity in the 1940s. Benny Goodman, Tommy Dorsey, and Duke Ellington were as likely to be playing on my stereo as were Cat Stevens, the Beatles, or Janis Joplin. I appreciated classical music, too. I'm grateful I was exposed to such a wide variety of musical styles. I'm sure that from somewhere deep within my mind the melodies, rhythms, chord changes, and lyrics I grew up with contribute to the songs I write today.

I've heard it said that we tend to write the kinds of songs we loved to listen to when we were in high school. That makes sense. Those are the songs that defined our tastes in music and so much more. They helped carve out our identity. The artists whom we admired as teenagers influenced how we dressed, who our friends were, and even our political leanings. So it's only natural that these are the artists whose music we would be influenced by.

But for some of my older students the problem is that Andy Williams, Perry Como, Connie Francis, the Andrews Sisters, and Doris Day are not currently looking for new songs to record. Likewise, for those of another generation, I don't hear current hits on the radio by artists who sound like Styx, Foreigner, the Temptations, Alice Cooper, Herman's Hermits, or Judy Collins.

Does this mean you shouldn't write these kinds of songs? No. Write what you love. Write what's in your heart. But if it sounds like something appropriate for a "Golden Oldies" show, accept that it probably won't be something you'll have commercial success with.

Often, when I ask my older students which current artists they envision recording their songs, they have no idea. "Casting" your songs is an important part of the process of taking care of business. When a publisher asks whom you think would be an appropriate artist for your song, be prepared with several answers. Remember that it's likely that numerous artists will pass on your song before it finds its home. Therefore, publishers typically look for the kinds of songs that could potentially be successful for many different artists.

Study your market. If you want to get your songs recorded in the Country music market but your idea of Country lies somewhere between the Carter Family, Roy Rogers, and Patsy Cline, you need to listen to current radio. Study the songs being recorded by artists like Faith Hill, Tim McGraw, the Dixie Chicks, Lonestar, and other contemporary Country music stars. Similarly, if you dream of Pop cuts but are unaware of the artists who are currently having hits with songs they did not write themselves, you're doing yourself and your songs a big disservice.

Listen to the radio stations that play current hits in the genres you want to write for and study the music charts. The radio is our greatest teacher, plus it's free and available twenty-four hours per day. Study what it's telling you. While you may not be moved to write for Jessica Simpson, Marc Anthony, or Santana, you may find outlets for your music with artists such as Lara Fabian, Andrea Bocelli, Sarah Brightman, Trisha Yearwood, Jim Brickman, Charlotte Church, or Celine Dion.

No one is forcing you to write songs that don't move you. But *if* your goal is to earn a living as a songwriter and to hear your songs on the radio, part of your job is finding an outlet for your work. Commercial music covers a wide spectrum, and if you make yourself aware of the range of possibilities, I'll bet you can find areas that you truly love—and where songs that come from your heart can find a good home.

Exercise

Take an hour or two each week to watch current hit videos. Don't just have them playing in the background. Really pay attention and familiarize yourself with the hot new artists. Make a list of those artists you'd like to write for. Listen to their albums and study the album liner notes, especially noting whether these artists record songs that were neither self-penned nor written by their producers. Then write a song that comes from your heart that would be perfect for each of these artists.

STAFF-WRITING

I signed my first staff-writing deal on May 24, 1991. I remember it well because it was one of the happiest moments of my life. Signing that document was the culmination of a dream that I'd begun dreaming more than eleven years earlier. It represented everything I wanted professionally: an opportunity to be paid to write songs; to quit the miserable day jobs; and to have a respected music publisher pitching my songs. It meant recognition of my talent, a chance to be professionally nurtured and groomed for a career as a successful songwriter, the credibility to collaborate with other professionals, and the first step toward fame and fortune.

A staff-writing deal is actually a misnomer. A staff-writer is not an employee of the publishing company and therefore receives none of the typical employee fringe benefits (i.e., health insurance or a pension plan). He or she is considered "self-employed" by the I.R.S. A staff-writing contract is actually an "Exclusive Publishing Agreement," and that's what it says on top of the contract. It means that during the term of the contract everything that an individual writes is automatically published by the company he or she is signed to.

As a staff-writer you have a quota of songs to deliver, usually between ten and fifteen per year if you write them alone. Double this amount if the songs are written with a collaborator. If your songs are the result of three-way collaborations, you would need to triple the number of songs you turn in to fulfill your contractual obligation. Exclusive publishing agreements typically include a clause requiring that your songs be "acceptable" to the publisher. While this doesn't mean that all of your songs are expected to be smash hits, it protects the publisher from a situation where you crank out a dozen substandard songs in a day just to fulfill your contractual obligation. Bear in mind, however, that being a successful staff-writer requires that your efforts produce income. If you write only three songs a year, but each of these songs becomes a Number One single, your staff-writing deal will be much more secure than if you turn in fifty, or even a hundred, songs that are "good," but fail to get recorded.

In exchange for granting the exclusive right to publish your songs, you are typically given an advance against your future mechanical royalties (income generated primarily by the sales of CDs, cassettes, and videos and synchronization licensing fees—monies paid to include music in movies and television shows). Not to be confused with a salary, a songwriter's advance is essentially a "loan" that your publisher will later recoup from your royalties.

The publisher also pays for the cost of recording demos and any costs incurred in pitching your songs (for example, postage and the cost of duplicating CDs). Depending on your level of clout, either all or a portion of the monies advanced to pay for producing demos and pitching songs may be recoupable.

If your songs are recorded and generate royalties from sales, your share of this income (known as the "writer's" share) is retained by your publisher and goes toward repaying the "debt" incurred when you took an advance against your own future mechanical royalties. Performance royalties, which are derived primarily from radio airplay and television broadcasts, are not usually applied toward recouping your advance.

When your staff-writing deal ends, if your songs have not generated sufficient income to repay the monies you've been advanced, you do not have to repay the publisher. However, unless otherwise negotiated, the publisher typically retains the publishing rights to all songs written during the time that you were under contract. If any songs you wrote during the term of your staff-writing deal generate mechanical royalties after your contract has expired, your share of these royalties will continue to be retained by the publisher until the company has recouped all monies advanced during the staff-writing deal.

When an exclusive publishing deal is signed, it is usually for a one-year period with several additional one-year options. These options to pick up the contract for additional years are the *publisher's* options—not the writer's. So, essentially, staff-writers are rarely guaranteed income for more than one year at a time.

It is in the publisher's best interests to secure as many option periods as the writer will agree to. Why? Because the publisher has no obligation to exercise these options; however, at the publisher's sole discretion, the writer may be committed to the company and locked in for a fixed amount of money for future years. If the writer becomes "hot," he or she is contractually bound to stay with the company at a time when that individual might be able to command a much higher financial advance and a better deal at another company. Of course, a smart publisher will renegotiate the contract to keep a "hot" writer happy.

When I signed my deal with Zomba, I was ecstatic that anyone was willing to pay to publish my songs. I would have happily granted them fifty one-year options and my firstborn, if they had asked. (That's why we have attorneys!) We settled on a one-year deal with three additional one-year options.

My first year, my advance was $13,000, plus a $5,000 bonus for bringing two-thirds of my share of the publishing rights to "Change My Mind," which had been recorded by the Oak Ridge Boys and was set to be released as a single. Note that until I had something concrete to bring to the table (the publishing rights to a song that was *already* recorded by a major artist), the staff-writing deal I wanted so desperately managed always to stay a step ahead of me.

I'd written "Change My Mind" with a great writer and super-nice guy named A.J. Masters. It was the first time I'd written with a Nashville staff-writer and the resulting song was by far the best song I had ever written. Later that night, when A.J. sang it for his wife Stephanie, she cried and said, "Our kids are going to college!" A.J.'s publisher, Bull's Creek Music, recorded a terrific demo of our song and three-and-a-half years later pitched it to the Oak Ridge Boys, who were still an enormously successful Country act back in 1991. Our song was set to follow a Number One single by the Oaks, so Zomba was relatively assured that they'd recoup their investment, and more.

For the three option periods, *if* Zomba chose to exercise my option, they would have to pay me a larger advance each year: $15,000 for the second year; $17,500 for the third year; and $22,500 for the fourth and final option period.

Well, my "sure thing" Oak Ridge Boys single stiffed big time. You've heard of a song having a bullet. Well, this turkey had an anchor! The recording was truly dreadful. The "harmonies" sounded like chalk on a board and the first time I heard it, I thought someone was playing a practical joke on me. Peaking at #70 on the *Billboard* Country Singles chart, I believe it was the lowest-charting single up to that point in the Oaks' illustrious career. I can laugh about it now but, believe me, it was devastating at the time.

During my first year as a staff-writer, I learned more than I ever imagined there was to learn about the craft of writing and marketing songs. My publisher walked me through the "Nashville" style of producing demos. I was hooked up with a variety of collaborators and my songs were put under the proverbial microscope. I had a couple of close calls, and even had a song recorded by a new artist who promptly lost her record deal before my song was ever released. But the bottom line was that since the Oak Ridge Boys disaster, I hadn't gotten any cuts and had not generated any income for my publisher.

Several months before the May 24 option renewal deadline approached, I became afflicted by a syndrome, *Contractrenewalaphobia*, that I would become far too familiar with in years to come. It included panic, anxiety, a pervasive sense of dread, and a nagging voice in the back of my head (that sounded suspiciously like my father) saying, "Oh my God, you're going to lose your staff-writing deal, which is all you ever wanted in the world, and now no other publisher will ever sign you again because they'll know that Zomba lost money on you and dropped you like a rock."

My fear began in late January. By mid-February it was really kicking, and by April it was so intense that I could barely concentrate long enough to write songs. A few weeks before May 24, the head of the company called me into his office. I wondered if he could see me shaking as he said that he believed in me as a writer but would not pay what he'd previously agreed in order to exercise my next year's option. I was reminded that the amount of my second-year advance had been negotiated based on the assumption that I'd have an Oak Ridge Boys hit that never materialized. He offered to pick up my option and keep me on for one more year, but at $10,500— almost one-third less than the $15,000 that had originally been negotiated. I could have wept with joy. I didn't care about the money. I had been given a reprieve, a chance to redeem myself, and surely I would have a huge hit by the following year.

This nightmare repeated itself with slight variations for the next four years. Most of those years, my advance remained at a whopping $10,500. So much for the Mercedes and the life of luxury. But bear in mind that staff-writers who have huge hits can command enormous advances. I was signed as a staff-writer for five-and-a-half years before the stars lined up just right and John Berry's version of "Change My Mind" became a big hit. Incredibly, at the same time, I hit the Top 40 on the Country charts with Steve Azar's "I Never Stopped Lovin' You," and had a single on both the Pop and R&B charts with J'Son's version of "I'll Never Stop Loving You," which went on to become a Number One R&B video and included in a Disney movie. An additional year went by before I saw significant income from those recordings.

I was very lucky to have signed with a publisher who believed in me enough to hang in for such a long time before I became successful and earned lots of money for the company. Unfortunately, that's a very rare situation. Typically, if a writer has not proven him or herself in the first year or two, he or she will be out looking for a new deal.

You may have already written the song that will open the door to your dreams. In the meantime, keep honing your skills so that when that door opens you'll be able to blow them away. But remember you've chosen a path that includes no guarantees of monetary rewards. If job security and financial stability are high on your priority list, be a lawyer or an accountant.

IT'S ALL WHO YOU KNOW

We've all heard the expression, "It's not *what* you know, but *who* you know" that matters when it comes to achieving success in the music business. There's a lot of truth to this statement. There's no doubt that it's important to have connections. But if you're serious about success, there's one person it's crucial that you get to know—yourself.

First, you need to be able to honestly assess your strengths and weaknesses. What areas do you excel in artistically, and what areas need some additional work? Do your melodies make listeners want to sing along, or move along? Do you come up with lyrical concepts that are fresh and inspiring, or are your words simply taking up space?

Next, you must assess how well you're handling the business side of the music biz. Are you doing all you need to do to get your music to the public? Are you maximizing your chances for success by networking, pursuing a publisher, performing (if you're also a singer), setting meetings with record label executives, becoming active in songwriter organizations, etc? Or are you too busy blaming your lack of success on the fact that you don't know the right people?

To be effective songwriters and singers, we need to be honest and real. Otherwise we're not artists, we're hacks. We need to be vulnerable, access the deepest parts of ourselves, and be willing to share what we find with millions of strangers. We can't do this if we don't know ourselves.

Examine those areas that you do well, and isolate those you need to improve. But don't use lack of contacts as an excuse for why you're not having the success you feel you deserve. Instead, use your time and energy to write great songs, make those contacts, and get to know a really neat person—you.

THE EGGS OF LOVE
(REVERSION CLAUSES)

I received a wonderful birthday gift this year—an e-mail from Jim Vellutato. You might recall from this book's chapter about rewriting that Jim was the music publisher responsible for getting my first cut. We'd lost touch over the years and having heard about my recent successes he was contacting me to congratulate me. Following the e-mail correspondence, we spoke over the phone. It felt great to be able to thank him and let him know what an important part he'd played in my development as a songwriter.

Our conversation reminded me of a song of mine that Jim had published in 1989. I'd written "The Edge of Love" with Ted Jacobs, a great guy who, at the time, was one of Jim's staff-writers at Famous Music in Los Angeles. This song represented a major leap and a considerable growth spurt for me as a writer. It was the first Pop song I'd written that made professionals sit up and take notice and, at the time, I was certain that it would be my first big hit.

Soon after writing "The Edge of Love," I attended a workshop where the special guest was Grammy-winning producer Michael Omartian (Christopher Cross, Rod Stewart, Amy Grant) and I gathered up the courage to introduce myself and offer him a copy of my song. Omartian was getting ready to produce Frances Ruffelle, a new artist on RCA Records who'd won a Tony Award for her performance on Broadway in *Les Miserables*, and I knew the song was perfect for her. When he politely refused to take my cassette, I remember feeling both hurt and angry that after all the work my collaborator and I had done writing this song and the money and effort we'd invested in producing the demo, he wouldn't even give me a chance. After all, this was a published song and I knew it was a hit waiting to happen.

Being persistent, I mailed the same song to Omartian's office but his assistant returned the package with a note saying they were not looking for material at this time—and had not listened to the song. However, when Jim Vellutato pitched the same song, being a reputable publisher, he had the clout to break through that invisible wall. The next thing I knew, my cowriter and I were invited to the studio while the vocals for our song were being recorded! I decided it would not be a great idea to mention to the producer that this was the same song he had refused to even listen to when I tried to give it to him—twice.

Frances' version of the song sounded fantastic. I could hardly believe how our simple, eight-track demo had been transformed into what felt like a full-blown radio hit. I was ecstatic to have reached another milestone in my career and I knew it was just a short matter of time until I'd be able to quit my job and be a rich and respected songwriter. But this story didn't have a happy ending. RCA decided not to release the album. Although the company had invested almost $200,000 in recording it, they didn't feel strongly enough about the finished product to invest the even-higher sums that would be necessary to successfully promote it. You might be surprised to learn how often this happens.

We managed to survive the disappointment and continued pitching the song, but with no luck. At one point, I sent a copy of "The Edge of Love" to a talent manager in New York, whom I'd learned from reading a tip sheet was looking for songs for one of her artists. Several weeks after I'd sent the song I made a follow-up call to ask the manager whether she'd had an opportunity to listen to "The Edge of Love." In a thoroughly shocked and indignant tone of voice she responded, "The *Eggs* of Love? Is this a joke? What kind of a crazy title is that?" (From that day on, my cowriter and I referred to our song as "The Eggs of Love—An Ovarian Chant.") We never did get a cut on that song, but we did get a good laugh and, as you'll see when you continue reading, I learned a very important lesson about reversion clauses.

Unless your contract specifies otherwise, when you publish a song the agreement remains in force forever. However, in many instances songwriters are able to secure a "reversion clause." When invoked, this provision causes all of the publisher's rights to a song to *revert* back to the writer after a specified length of time, if particular criteria are not met. For example, if the song has not been commercially released on a major label (as defined in the contract), or included in a major film or television show within three years, the writer has the right to terminate the publishing agreement. Some publishers refuse to include this or a similar clause in their agreement, but many will—and it is something that any competent entertainment attorney will request. (You should *always* have an entertainment attorney review any publishing or recording contract before signing it.)

Of course, it's in a publisher's best interests to keep the song for as long as possible before it reverts back to the writer. This provides a longer window of opportunity to place the song with an artist or in a film or television show. When granting a reversion clause, publishers typically request a two- or three-year period, citing that it often takes that long for a song to find its home. Even five years is not unheard of.

Conversely, it's in the writer's best interest to have a shorter amount of time (one or two years) specified in the reversion clause. The Songwriters Guild of America (SGA) has a sample contract available at their website (**www.songwriters.org**) which is drafted to be fair to all parties while ensuring that the songwriters' best interests are served. SGA recommends a one-year reversion period, at the end of which the publisher has the right to pay $250 to extend the agreement for an additional six months.

Bear in mind that if a publisher has advanced you any money, or paid any expenses on your behalf (demo costs, copyright fees, etc.) you will probably have to repay this before the rights revert to you. If your publisher has not secured a commercially released recording within the time period specified in the contract, but is continuing to work hard to promote your song, it would probably be good business to extend the contract for an additional six months or a year, without requiring any payment.

Sometimes it takes a long time for an album to be released after the songs have been recorded. At the end of the time stated in your reversion clause, if a publisher is either on the verge of securing a recording or has secured a recording that is pending release, it would be unethical (albeit legal) to demand that the rights revert back to you. The music business is a relatively small one, and you don't want to burn any bridges.

When we sign a publishing contract, we hope and anticipate that it will lead to the publisher's efforts generating lots of money from our songs. If this were not our expectation, we wouldn't be signing the agreement. However, things don't always work out the way we hope—especially in the music business. Including a reversion clause in your contract is the best protection against your song sitting on a shelf and collecting dust (instead of royalties) in the event that the company that signed it goes out of business; the person who loved your song and offered you the publishing contract leaves the company and the new publisher doesn't like it; or, after a few months, the publisher who swore your song was "a guaranteed smash" is no longer excited about the song and has stopped pitching it.

Bear in mind that unless otherwise specified, your publisher is entitled to fifty percent of any monies your song generates, regardless of who actually is responsible for getting the song recorded during the term of your contract. This means that if you, or your collaborator, or anyone else places your song into Janet Jackson's hand and she records it, your publisher still collects the publisher's fifty percent of the income.

My contract with Famous Music to publish "The Edge of Love" included a reversion clause that specified that the publishing rights to the song would revert back to me after three years, if the song had not been commercially released on a major label within that period of time. Although the song had been recorded, it had not been *released*—nor was it going to be. By reimbursing Famous Music for the $250 they had advanced for my share of the demo costs, I was able to reclaim the publishing rights to my song. Jim Vellutato is still a very successful music publisher, but he's long since left Famous. Thanks to my attorney's insisting on a reversion clause, I'm now free to publish the song elsewhere or retain the publishing rights myself.

ONLY THE BEST

I demoed six new songs last week. Immediately after mixing them, instead of leaving the studio and compulsively playing my new songs over and over and over (and over) again as I typically would, I sped to the airport and left to work out of town. I didn't want to travel with my only copy of the master recording, so I left it at home. Ten days elapsed before I could hear my babies.

When I listened to the songs with a fresh, objective ear, my suspicions were confirmed. Out of the six new songs I was pretty certain that one was a standout—a "Wow," that I'd likely get recorded. One other song was very strong and might have a shot. That meant that the remaining four songs missed the mark.

I had worked hard on each of these songs. I'd played rough work tapes for my publisher so he could lend his expertise and I rewrote the songs to incorporate his suggestions. He thought they were good and so did I, as did my cowriters and their respective publishers. Otherwise, we wouldn't have invested in demos.

I did my very best when recording each of the demos, planning out arrangements, hiring the best musicians, engineer, studio, and singers that I could afford. I put in a couple of fourteen-hour days, spent several sleepless nights obsessing, and poured one hundred and ten percent of my heart and soul into each one of these songs. Now the final verdict was that only one out of the six was exceptional—and one additional song was straddling the border between "better than good" and "I've got to cut that song." Those other four songs were only "good"—a euphemism for "worthless" in a business where only the very strongest have a prayer of rising to the top.

My initial feeling was that I had failed myself, my songs, and my collaborators; that I had wasted time and money on songs that were not likely to ever generate income. But then I put down the whip and started thinking about the fact that I had written and demoed at least *one* exceptional song that would have a good chance of getting recorded; a song that I truly loved, that would blow people away. That's something I only dreamed of when I began my songwriting journey. If I could consistently write an extraordinary song one out of every six times I sat down to work, I'd probably carve out an amazing career.

Something a professional photographer once told me comes to mind. She said that when she does a photo session, she typically takes three rolls of film with thirty-six exposures on each roll; more than one hundred pictures. She considers the shoot a success if she gets one or two great photos out of the batch. Those other pictures aren't "failures." They're part of process that leads to success.

On a whim I looked up "best" in the dictionary. Webster defined it as the "superlative" of good; of the "highest" quality or standing. While many can be of "high" quality, by definition only one can be the "highest."

It's great to aim high. That's how our writing improves. But painful as it might be, we have to accept that every song we write can't be our best. We have to write them anyway, trusting that each song brings us closer to our goals.

GOD, GRANT ME THE SERENITY. . .

The years I spent working at RCA Records gave me an incredible education. In some instances, though, I learned things about the inner workings of a record label that I wished I never knew. I'll never forget how shocked I was while working in the Country promotion department when I heard my boss tell a radio programmer to stop playing one of our songs that we'd previously been begging him to play.

Let me get this straight. The music programmer at the radio station wanted to play the song and their listeners wanted to hear it, but the record label told them not to. Why? Because each mainstream radio station has a limited playlist—typically not more than forty songs, and sometimes as few as twenty or thirty.

If the promotion department at the record label has a clear indication that a certain song is meeting resistance from many of the radio programmers, and is unlikely to do well, they will likely ask the stations that are playing this song to drop it from their playlists, thereby opening up an additional slot for a song that the label feels may have a better shot of becoming a hit.

Well, now it makes perfect sense, but when I learned this lesson I was horrified and couldn't help but put myself into the shoes of the writer who'd written that song. I was well on my way to learning how much more goes into the success of a song than just writing a good song. The information that follows will make a lot more sense if I explain how a song becomes Number One (or any other number) on *Billboard's* or another publication's charts.

Although the average listener might never realize it, the current singles that get played throughout the day are not randomly chosen. While the DJ might mix in a few "oldies" and requests at his or her discretion, the current songs that are included on the playlist are determined by the music director or program director. In many instances, this decision, which is so crucial to a song's and artist's success, is made by a consultant who has been hired by the radio station. Corporations that own numerous radio stations often assign the same playlist to all of their stations.

Based on the decision of the music director, program director, or consultant, some of the songs on this list get played more frequently than others. Those that receive the most airplay are considered in "heavy" rotation; those receiving fewer "spins" per day are listed in "medium rotation"; while those songs receiving the least amount of daily airplay are in "light" rotation.

Two primary publications compile charts of current singles. These are *Billboard* and *R&R (Radio & Records)*. A small number of the most successful radio stations in the U.S. in each musical format (i.e., Pop, Country, Urban, Jazz, Christian, etc.) become designated as "reporting" stations by the publications that maintain music charts. These stations report their playlists to the above publications and let them know when they have added a new single, as well as how much airplay each song is receiving (i.e., light, medium, or heavy rotation). The record labels have promoters on staff and frequently augment their efforts by hiring "independent promoters" who primarily target the reporting stations to encourage them to add songs to their playlists, or to move them into heavier rotation.

Each song is assigned a numerical point value based on the amount of airplay it's receiving at the reporting stations. These numbers form the basis of chart position. A Number One Pop or Country song will typically be played between seven and eight thousand times per week—counting only those stations that are designated as "reporters." When you add in airplay on the hundreds of additional radio stations that do not report their playlists to *Billboard* or *R&R*, a hit single will likely be played hundreds of thousands of times. Over the course of many years, songs that become "standards" typically are played more than a million times.

The *Billboard* Hot 100 Singles Pop chart positions are based on a combination of airplay and sales figures. However, in Country music many songs are not available as commercial singles, so the chart position is based solely on airplay as reported by the reporting stations. All of the *R&R* charts are based exclusively on airplay. Since entire albums do not receive airplay (only those songs released as singles), the *Billboard* album charts are based exclusively on sales figures.

A song receives a "bullet" on the chart to designate that it has gained additional airplay and/or sales since the previous week on a station's list. By reading *R&R* (or subscribing to it online), you can actually see a listing of the playlists of reporting stations throughout the country. You can monitor which songs have been added or dropped in any given week, as well as how much airplay a given song is receiving at any reporting station.

Armed with this information, when I've had singles on the charts, I could hardly wait to see the latest issue of *R&R*. I'd pounce on it when it was delivered to my publisher's office each Thursday afternoon. I watched my single's progress with baited breath, and noted how many stations were playing it, which ones had just added it to their playlists, and which ones were moving it into heavier or (God forbid) lighter rotation.

There was a point when John Berry's version of my song "Change My Mind" was being played by more than ninety-five percent of the reporting stations. I needed those stations that were holding out to play the song or it would have no chance of reaching the Number One position. I've never been the kind of guy who can calmly sit back and wait. I didn't know if it would be effective, but I had to do something.

So, I sent faxes to the music directors and program directors of those stations that were not yet playing my song. I included facts that I hoped would persuade them to add the song to their playlists. For example, I sent quotes from radio stations that were reporting a huge number of telephone requests for the song, a copy of the *Billboard* Country sales chart showing that it was the Number Two-selling Country single in the nation, and a list of other successful stations in their area that were playing the song. I asked them to listen to the song one more time and to seriously consider playing it.

Did my efforts help? I'll never know for sure, but at least I did whatever I felt I could do. Eventually, every reporting station played my song. Unfortunately, before the last stations added it, a couple of the early believers who had been playing the song from the beginning of its release dropped it from their lists. So it never received enough points at one time to go to the top of the charts. But I was ecstatic when I saw it reach the Top Ten on every major chart, and the #4 position in *R&R*.

This story began by my relating how I felt as I watched a song being "killed" by the record label. The lives of the writers of that song were changed in that moment, and there was nothing they could do about it. So what can we as creative artists do about this and other situations that are out of our control, which we may, or may not, even be privy to?

The "Serenity Prayer" popular in Alcoholics Anonymous and other twelve-step programs comes to mind:

> God, grant me the serenity to accept the things I cannot change. Courage to change the things I can. And the wisdom to know the difference.

As songwriters, what can we change—and what do we have to accept?

Songwriters typically are not invited to the studio when their songs are being recorded. I have no control over the way the artist sings, the way the players play, or the way the producer produces. How effectively the promoters promote the song and the response it receives from radio listeners are also not within the realm of my control. So, it's not productive for me to get crazy over these things. Of course, that's often easier said than done.

As a songwriter, though, I *can* make time for my creativity and nurture it. I can take classes, read books, hone my craft, and write the very best songs I'm capable of. I can tweak the melodies and put the lyrics under the proverbial microscope. I can be like a dog with a bone and not let go until I've gotten it just right. Then I can get professional input and critiques from publishers or songwriting teachers and rewrite my songs to make them even better. I can invest in the very highest quality demo I can afford to illustrate my song's potential and express my vision for it. I can network, go to workshops where industry professionals will be present, do my best to secure meetings, and distribute copies of my songs to individuals with the power to say, "Yes."

Occasionally I get lucky and I secure a recording of my "baby." But then it's out of my hands. I can't control luck or fate—whether I'm going to run into the head of Atlantic Records at the mall, or whether Aerosmith is going to be on my flight. But luck has a habit of visiting those who don't depend on it, and fate seems to smile upon those who work hard and are prepared to deliver when the opportunity presents itself.

All I can do is the very best that I'm capable of in those areas I can control, wish on a star, hope for the best—and accept the results. Then I can go write an even better song.

Exercise

Purchase a copy of *Billboard* magazine and *R&R (Radio and Records)*. Read the albums and singles charts and become familiar with the symbols. Watch the progress of your favorite song, noting:

- ✓ Who wrote this song? (Was it written by the artist, the producer, or an "outside" songwriter?)
- ✓ How many weeks did it take for this song to reach its peak chart position?
- ✓ Has this song (or the album it's included on) been certified gold or platinum?
- ✓ Who publishes the song?

Now, close your eyes and imagine your song rising up the chart!

SEPTEMBER 11, 2001

I guess none of us will ever forget where we were when we first learned the news that hijacked planes had crashed into the World Trade Center and the Pentagon. I had finished teaching at the West Coast Songwriters Association (formerly the Northern California Songwriters Association)* Conference the previous day, and decided to take my rental car and spend a couple of days relaxing in the Wine Country. That's where I was when I turned on the morning news as the horror was still in the midst of unfolding.

The images on television seemed so much like a movie that I could barely comprehend their truth. It quickly became clear that I was not going to be able to fly back home the next day as I had planned. The fact that I was now stranded more than two thousand miles from home added to the sense of surrealism.

I decided to make the best of the situation and, although my heart wasn't in it, I did some sightseeing. At least I wasn't stuck in an airport. I had credit cards, a little bit of cash, and the realization that the minor inconvenience I was suffering was negligible compared to the nightmare that so many people were enduring.

The next day, while walking along a rugged trail on a bluff above the Pacific, the last thing on my mind was songwriting. In fact, I was having a hard time imagining how I'd be able to go back to writing love songs in a few days while buildings, lives, and the sense of our world being a relatively safe place to live were crumbling. Writing songs suddenly seemed hopelessly insignificant.

As I looked at the coastline that stretched below me, an uninvited thought popped into my head. I recognized it as the beginning of a song idea. I didn't want to write a song, but the melody insisted on being heard and the words came forth as if they had a will of their own:

---

* For information about the West Coast Songwriters Association visit **www.westcoastsongwriters.org**

97

I pray for the ones who feel a cause
is more important than a life
And I grieve for the innocence
that's disappeared like a thief in the night
And I believe that we'll be shown a way
To find a promise of love in the shadows of hate

I wondered how many of the other writers who had attended the conference were experiencing the same phenomenon. Would other writers' grief and sadness be expressed in song? The answer came when I returned to my hotel room and checked e-mails on my laptop. One writer had sent the lyrics to John Lennon's "Imagine." Several others had forwarded lyrics they had written that were inspired by the crisis. When I checked phone messages there was an *a capella* song about the tragedy. In the week that followed the attacks I received more than ten lyrics from writers throughout the U.S. and from as far away as India. I wasn't alone.

As I watched the memorial services on television, experiencing the power of "Amazing Grace" and "God Bless America," it was clear that there's nothing insignificant about what we do. Songs help us express and identify our feelings; they also provide catharsis. As songwriters, we give listeners the words they wish they could say—and those they long to hear. Our music provides a reason to dance and to sing.

Wars have always inspired deep emotions in writers. When songwriters are moved, they write songs. "The Star Spangled Banner" was inspired by the War of 1812. Whitney Houston's version of it was played regularly following the Gulf War and again after the September 11, 2001 attack. World War II gave us the Andrews Sisters' "Boogie Woogie Bugle Boy." The Vietnam conflict motivated writers to express their feelings about the war from the protests of Country Joe and the Fish's "I Feel Like I'm Fixin' to Die Rag" (Remember, "1-2-3- What Are We Fightin' For?") to the unabashed patriotism of "The Ballad of the Green Berets."

Whether our creativity expresses a teenager's feelings about first love, a gangsta rapper's rage at society's injustices, our grief over this brutal attack on our country, or any other political issue or cause, our songs are important. Personally, I'm grateful to have been given the gift of sharing my feelings and observations about the world.

INDEPENDENT PLUGGERS

I might not have a career as a songwriter today if it were not for the efforts of an independent songplugger I worked with back in 1995. Liz Rose (who has since blossomed into a wonderful, successful songwriter) was responsible for pitching my song "Change My Mind," (written with A.J. Masters) for John Berry. That cut resulted in a Top Five Country single for me at a time when I was a breath away from losing my staff-writing deal with Zomba.

I'd had a meeting with Mike Hollandsworth, who at the time was the head of Zomba's Nashville office. I'd been told that since I had failed to generate hits or appreciable income during my five years signed to the company, the professional relationship was clearly not working for me, or for the company. He said that when my contract expired he would not be picking up my option. In other words I was being fired.

This was my worst nightmare. I was panicking, watching my dreams slip away. But I somehow managed to say that I knew deep in my heart—as clearly as I'd ever known anything—that I was about to have great success. And that I knew I was supposed to have that success at Zomba.

I groveled and begged, and Mike took pity, agreeing to extend my contract for six more months, with a $5,000 total advance to live off of during that time. But the understanding was that if I didn't get a hit during the next six months, my deal would not be renewed—and there would be no more pleading, begging, or discussion.

Earning only $833 per month, I didn't have much money but I kept expenses low by renting a room in a converted attic. I used a good portion of my income to hire an independent plugger to augment my publisher's efforts, with the hope that I would get a big cut—quickly. It worked. Getting that hit as a result of Liz's efforts earned me my first "Gold" record (an award that acknowledges sales of 500,000 copies in the U.S.) and lots of money. Seeing that symbol of accomplishment hanging on my wall was worth far more to me than any money.

Getting that hit at that point in time allowed me to keep my deal with Zomba for an additional seven years, until the company was absorbed by corporate giant Bertelsmann Music Group (BMG). Being at Zomba led directly to my getting cuts with Britney Spears and the Backstreet Boys many years later. Those cuts generated an enormous amount of money for me, as well as credibility and career opportunities that money couldn't buy.

So, am I recommending that everyone rush out and hire an independent songplugger? Before I answer that, I want to define the functions of a songplugger and discuss the difference between an independent plugger and a song publisher.

While both pluggers and publishers are in business to get songs recorded, an independent songplugger is an individual who represents songs for a fee—as opposed to a publisher, whose payment comes in the form of the publisher's share of any royalties the songs might generate.

An independent plugger typically earns the majority of his or her living by charging a fee in the form of a monthly retainer. This amount varies widely and is based primarily on the plugger's credits and how many of your songs will be represented, as well as how many additional writers' catalogs he or she is handling. Pluggers typically represent many writers simultaneously so that they can earn enough money to maintain an office and pay themselves. The monthly fee to retain a songplugger varies considerably but typically ranges from $200–$1,000 per month.

Pluggers get paid their monthly fee whether you get a cut or not. But publishers earn money *only* if their songs generate income. This typically occurs when a publisher (or writer) successfully places a song with a recording artist, in a film, or on a television show, thereby generating royalties or licensing fees.

Reputable publishers *never* charge writers a fee to publish songs. Similarly, legitimate record labels never charge money to review material or include it on an album. The only fee you might incur when working with a legitimate publisher would be reasonable costs to produce demos of your songs. But, typically, a publisher will pay for these costs and recoup them from any future royalties your songs might generate.

Independent pluggers usually are also paid a "bonus" in the event that they secure a recording or otherwise generate income from a song. The bonus is typically based upon how many copies of the song are sold, and in the event that it's a single, how high the song goes on the charts.

Some pluggers request higher monthly retainers and lower bonuses, while others might be willing to work for little or even no up-front money, but much higher bonuses in the event they secure a cut. Of course it's to the writer's advantage to pay as little as possible up front, because it minimizes his or her financial risk, as well as giving the plugger additional incentive to generate cuts. The amounts listed on the sample bonus schedule that follows are negotiable and might be considerably higher or lower depending on factors including the monthly retainer being paid and the plugger's track record.

SAMPLE BONUS SCHEDULE
FOR POP, R&B, AND COUNTRY CUTS

FOR ALBUM CUTS:

$500 to be paid upon U.S. release of a major label album cut

In addition:

- $2,500 to be paid if the album is certified "Gold" in the U.S. (500,000 units sold)
- Total of $5,000 to be paid if the album is certified "Platinum" (1,000,000 units sold)
- Additional $2,500 to be paid for each additional one million units sold

FOR SINGLE RELEASES:

(Fees are in addition to payments for album release and sales bonuses. All chart positions refer to *Billboard's* U.S. singles charts.)

- $2,500 total to be paid if the single peaks between the #40 – 31 position
- $3,500 total to be paid if the single peaks between the #30 – 21 position
- $5,000 total to be paid if the single peaks between the #20 – 11 position
- $7,500 total to be paid if the single peaks between the #10 – 5 position
- $10,000 total to be paid if the single peaks between the #4 – 1 position
- Additional $5,000 to be paid for each week beyond the first week that the single remains at #1.

(The amounts listed above are not cumulative)

The figures on this bonus schedule are provided as ballpark figures, and apply only to "mainstream" releases—meaning Pop, Country, Adult Contemporary, or R&B/Urban music. Songs recorded in other genres (i.e., Christian, Jazz, Blues, Cabaret, Bluegrass, Comedy, or Folk) typically receive only a fraction of the airplay and sales of mainstream songs, and therefore earn much less money and would require a different agreement. Some independent pluggers agree to be paid a percentage (typically 15%–20%) of any income their efforts might generate. This percentage might, or might not, be in addition to a monthly retainer.

You can see that using this bonus schedule, an independent plugger who secured a Number One single that was included on a Platinum-selling album would earn:

$500 for the initial album release
+ $5,000 when the album was certified Platinum
+ an additional $10,000 when the single went to Number One
Total: $15,500, in addition to whatever monies were collected from the monthly retainer

While this may seem like an exorbitant amount of money to pay, remember: one hundred percent of nothing equals nothing. Bear in mind that if the writer of this song had written the song with one cowriter, and did not own his or her own publishing rights, it's likely that he or she would have earned:

$20,000 in mechanical royalties (for 1,000,000 units sold in the U.S.)
+ approximately $100,000 in performance royalties
Total: $120,000*

If the writer was the sole writer and owned his or her share of the publishing rights, this figure would be quadrupled.

So now that you understand the nuts and bolts (not to mention how much money a hit song can earn), should you hire an independent plugger? Here's my take: If your songs are so strong that you could easily attract a reputable publisher, or if you are already signed with a publisher and want a little extra help pitching your songs, then an

---

*This figure is based on a mechanical royalty rate of 8.00 cents per unit. This rate will increase to 8.50 cents on January 1, 2004 and 9.10 cents effective January 1, 2006. For a detailed discussion of songwriting royalties and publishing refer to Chapters 11, 12, and 13 of 6 *Steps to Songwriting Success.*

indie plugger may be just the ticket for you. On the other hand, if you're thinking about hiring an independent plugger because you can't find a publisher who believes in your songs, it probably won't work.

It's incredibly tough for anyone to get songs recorded in this highly competitive market. If your songs are anything less than exceptional (not just "good"), paying someone to pitch them won't get them recorded by legitimate artists. If your songs are indeed exceptional, you should be able to find publishers who will recognize their merit and be willing to pitch them for free—in exchange for a portion of the royalties that will be generated in the event that they secure a recording.

Finding a publisher is not easy, but if your songs are "Wow" and you network and take care of business, you should be able to attract one's attention. Of course, it's much easier to pay someone to represent your songs, but it will rarely be effective unless your songs are at a level where they can compete with, and beat out, those that are written by staff-writers for those coveted slots on major albums.

I've seen too many of my students who are aspiring to be professional writers throw away thousands of dollars by paying a monthly retainer to pluggers to represent their songs. These writers believe their songs are hits and are willing to put their money where their mouths are. I respect that. But I have not yet seen even one of them secure a legitimate recording as a result of their efforts. Why? Because their songs are "good," but not yet "great"—and the competition is tough.

In order to be effective, independent pluggers need to represent only the highest-caliber songs and writers. Their reputations, credibility, and ability to successfully do business are contingent on delivering a hit, or at least a serious contender, when they play songs at those hard-to-get meetings with the decision makers. If they play songs that are less than stellar, those doors will be locked tight next time.

Typically, the best pluggers will represent only a small, elite group of established writers. That's how they keep those doors open. If you're wondering why successful, published writers would need a songplugger, it all comes down to looking for an edge in an incredibly competitive business.

If my publisher schedules a meeting to play songs for a major producer, that producer might be willing to listen to only eight songs during this meeting. In addition to me, there are fifteen successful writers signed to the publishing company. I might have at least three songs that I think would be perfect for the artists this producer is working with. You do the math. If I'm lucky, I might get one song played for this producer. An independent plugger can add to my publisher's efforts.

Unfortunately, as in any business, there are some unscrupulous independent songpluggers who prey on unsuspecting writers' hopes, dreams, and belief in their songs. In order to be represented by these pluggers, the only thing you need to be able to write is a monthly check.

These sharks know they will never place the songs they represent and are not anticipating receiving bonuses. They earn their living by collecting monthly retainers from a slew of hopeful, amateur writers. Before long, their reputations precede them and they are not able to get meetings with the people who are in a position to place songs with major artists. While they may provide monthly lists of all the places your songs were pitched, these songs are typically dropped off and relegated to the pile of songs received from non-professionals, where they sit until trash day arrives. Hopefully, there's a special little corner in hell for these scumbags where they can spend eternity having to listen to disco versions of the songs written by the writers they've taken advantage of.

When deciding whether an independent songplugger might be a wise investment for you, remember that if you've tried hard, but can't find a publisher who believes your songs will beat out the competition, it's extremely unlikely that an independent songplugger will be able to get your songs cut just because you're paying him or her a monthly retainer.

If you do decide to employ the services of an indie plugger, be sure to find someone who is reputable and effective. You might start by getting referrals from other songwriters or performing rights organizations. Politely asking your prospective plugger some important questions will not make you seem difficult to work with. You will come across as a professional. Remember, you're hiring *them*. It's appropriate to request monthly updates, specifying which songs have been pitched, whether these songs were played at face-to-face meetings (as opposed to being mailed or dropped off), and what comments and responses were received.

Before entering into an agreement with a songplugger, ask how many writers he or she is currently representing. Who are these other writers and do they have professional credits? What cuts has the plugger personally been responsible for and what music business connections does he or she have? What specific plans does he or she have for pitching your songs? By the way, these are also appropriate questions to ask a publisher before signing your songs. I strongly suggest getting confirmation that the information you receive is true.

Because of the intensely competitive nature of the music business, anything we can do to gain an edge over our competition should be considered. But remember that without exceptional songs it won't matter who is representing them.

REACTION SONGS

Last New Year's Day I had an epiphany. I was thinking about my goals for the coming year and what steps I could take to achieve them when suddenly it became crystal clear to me: I needed to give the decision makers (i.e., publishers, record label execs, producers, and recording artists) compelling reasons to select *my* song, instead of one of the hundreds of others being pitched for any given project.

It seems so obvious to me now, but at the time this was a revelation. It hit me that after all the years I had spent as a staff-writer, I had learned the rules of the game and the songs I wrote were perfectly crafted. But so were the hundreds of others in consideration. Why should an artist choose my song over one written by her producer, best friend, lover, boyfriend, husband, mother—or herself?

I realized that my job was to create songs that were not just "good," but those that stood above the crowd—songs that were special. If I wanted someone to choose my songs, I'd have to write songs that were significantly better than those the artist could write himself, or those that he could find within his inner circle.

This point got hammered home powerfully when I recently received an e-mail from my publisher's New York office that included a list of the artists for whom they were currently looking for songs. At the bottom of the page it said that in all instances they were looking for "Reaction Songs." Then it went on to explain what that meant.

It said that a Reaction Song was one that moved the listener to take some kind of action, the kind of song that causes the station's phone lines to light up like fireworks when it's played on the radio, with listeners calling in to say, "Who was that artist?" "I love that song." "Please play that song again and dedicate it to my boyfriend." "How can I get a copy of that song?" Reaction Songs elicit the kind of response that causes listeners to rush out to their local stores and buy the album and to ask their friends, "Have you heard that great new song?"

So, how can we accomplish this? The first step is to learn the basics—successful song structures, those elements that make melodies memorable, and how to write lyrics that communicate what you intend. Once you've accomplished this it's time to get to the next level. When the initial creative burst is over and you have a rough draft of a song, then it's time to get tough. Look for how you can make it more unique, more special, more "Wow."

Sometimes the answer includes using rhythms that are a little quirkier, or replacing a cliché line of lyric with one that pushes the envelope. Other times we may need to reshape a melody, making it less predictable but more memorable. Maybe the title and concept need to be fresher, an angle that hasn't been done before. Possibly the song could benefit from an unexpected note or chord, a "magic moment" that would grab the listener's attention.

When you've done the best work you're capable of to distinguish your song from the pack, reflect its uniqueness in your demo. Think "outside the box," using sounds, instrumentation, and musical approaches that would cause a listener to take notice.

Yesterday, when I played a new demo for my Nashville publishers, I was a little nervous because I had pushed the envelope further than I ever had for a Country song. The demo really rocked and sounded more like something Sheryl Crow or Melissa Etheridge might sing than anything I could pitch for Reba McEntire or Martina McBride. But my publishers were excited about the song. One of them, Lynn Gann, said that A&R people listen to songs all day long and that we've got to grab their attention and give them something that will "snap them out of their A&R trance." (The same thing certainly applies to publishers.)

The bottom line is that to succeed in an extremely competitive field, we have to find ways to set our songs apart. Finishing ten more perfectly crafted songs won't get you the same attention as writing one song that's truly innovative—a unique concept built with truly fresh, original melodies, lyrics, and rhythms.

Artists know that entire careers are built upon exceptional songs. Would Britney Spears have become a superstar if there had never been "… Baby One More Time?" Look what "I Hope You Dance" did for Lee Ann Womack and how "Amazed" skyrocketed Lonestar to superstardom. These are what are often referred to as "career singles," meaning songs that establish an artist's career or propel it to a next level. It's incredibly difficult for a new artist to break through and become a household name. Study the songs that were artists' first hits and ask yourself what tools and techniques the writers used to make these songs special enough to take an unknown artist all the way to Number One. Some of these songs include "It Wasn't Me" for Shaggy, "There Is No Arizona" for Jamie O'Neal, "Genie in a Bottle" for Christina Aguilera, "When Sunny Came Home" for Shawn Colvin, "A Thousand Miles" for Vanessa Carlton, and "Livin' La Vida Loca" for Ricky Martin.

"Good" is not good enough. If we're going to beat the competition we've got to write the kinds of songs that will compel an artist to say, "This song will be a Number One hit, a Grammy winner. It will take my career to the next level, and I've got to bump my own song off of this album to record this other one because it's so exceptional." Snap them out of their trances by writing Reaction Songs and give them a reason to say "Yes."

Exercise

Think about the last time a song made a powerful impression on you, exciting you enough to tell someone about it or to go out and buy it. Listen to the song and answer the following questions:

- ✓ What is it that I love about this song?
- ✓ What sets it apart from other songs of its type?
- ✓ What is it about the lyrical concept of this song that's fresh and original?
- ✓ What melodic techniques did the writer use (including chord and rhythm choices) to craft a melody that is unique and memorable?

See what happens when you incorporate some of these tools into the next song you write.

I AM NOT A MACHINE

I *should* be writing more songs. I *should* be writing better songs. I *should* be setting more appointments to pitch my songs. I *should* be networking and expanding my circle of collaborators. I *should* be performing more. Or practicing guitar. Or studying the latest hits. The list is endless.

It's not productive to "should" on ourselves. But I admit I've beaten myself up a thousand times or more for not doing enough to advance my career. Sometimes, I've dared to go to a movie or read a book instead of writing, rewriting, or pitching songs. Other times, I've watched mindless television when I "should" have been doing something to further my career. Many of these times, however, I've found that somewhere around 11:00 p.m. a song effortlessly poured out of me.

Yesterday was a Sunday and I spent most of the day in bed, watching a movie and reading magazines. That's rare for me and I chastised myself for being lazy. Today, I went for a walk at Radnor Lake and could barely contain the ideas that were pouring out of me. I don't think it would have happened if I had pushed myself when I was exhausted the previous day. We need to replenish emotionally, as well as physically. (I crave a lot of water when I write. I think it's my body's attempt to replace all of the concentrated energy I'm expending.)

Songwriting as a profession is intensely competitive and it's hard to justify taking time off to relax when your competition may be writing a hit song. It's difficult to find a balance, especially when you have to work a day job and maintain relationships, as well as juggle the additional responsibilities of everyday life.

The nature of songwriting is such that it's difficult to define what is "enough." If I were an accountant and had a huge pile of paperwork to complete, when I had finished the last calculation I'd know I was through. What's enough for a songwriter? A Top Ten hit? A Number One? Ten million units sold? Fifty million?

The truth, I suspect, is that whatever I achieve, it will never be enough. If I were named "Songwriter of the Year" I'd want to sustain it the following year—and then the year after that. If I won a Grammy I'd want another, and then another, because part of me is still trying to use success to fill up a hole that can't be filled by hit songs or the money they earn. I was a miserable kid in high school, an overweight outcast who was picked on and made fun of. I was "sensitive," preferring music and writing poetry to the more socially acceptable activities such as sports. I paid the price for being different.

Now, more than twenty-five years later, being inducted into my high school alumni "Hall of Fame" was in some ways almost as satisfying as winning a Grammy. The kid I was in high school was really hurting inside—although he would have denied it vehemently at the time. He wanted to be accepted and well liked. The taunting and physical abuse left their invisible scars.

When I received a standing ovation from more than a thousand people in the very same high school auditorium where so many times I had felt shame and self-loathing, on some level, that teenager who still lives inside of me was vindicated. He was able to see that it really was okay to be different; that he didn't have to be a football jock in order to make a valuable contribution. I wish he had believed that back then. Life is funny. Those kids who laughed at me in high school have grown up and some of them have probably bought my Britney Spears and Backstreet Boys records for their kids.

I suspect that the need to prove myself, to show that I'm good enough, fueled the drive that kept me working in the face of so much rejection. The years have brought much more self-acceptance, but on some level there's still a teenager inside of me who's trying to win approval from his peers—and from his Dad. For that kid, I'm not sure there will ever be enough gold records.

Success and acknowledgment can be wonderful, and I hope you'll experience them. But the reality is that commercial recognition is something we won't all attain. Besides, it's just a temporary fix for those old wounds. Give that kid inside of you a hug and tell him he's okay "as is," whether his (or her) songs are ever on the charts or not. 'Cause that's the truth.

CREATIVITY

Twice in the past week interviewers have asked me where my creativity and inspiration come from. As I thought about this during my morning walk, I realized that I can't imagine *not* creating. It's such a natural part of who I am.

I think we all have within us the drive to create. It's part of the definition of being human. We're constantly "creating" our perception of our environment, filtering and organizing stimuli. Our imaginations work nonstop. We generate new ideas constantly—even in our sleep. It's really amazing when you think about it: we're creation machines.

I don't profess to be a spiritual giant, but I do have some thoughts about the relationship between creativity and spirituality. We're all parts of the ongoing process of creation. The ultimate Creator fashioned us with unlimited capacity to create new thoughts and ideas. To me, that makes our creativity part of something bigger and sacred; it's something to be respected, revered, and honored.

For some of us, the impulse to create might manifest as a desire to sing, write poems, or paint. Others might be drawn to dance, sculpt, compose songs, or design jewelry. But most of us don't fully tune in to our creative self and allow it to surface because we're afraid we won't be good enough. That's the message we get from parents and society. But I believe the act of creation itself is important and valuable, even if what results from that creation neither gets critically acknowledged nor generates income. It's true that every person who wants to be an actor, writer, artist, or singer won't make money from their art. But that's not the only way to measure success.

So, what inspires me? Being in a tranquil natural setting. I love walking in the woods, in the mountains, or along the beach. I've gotten some of my most creative thoughts when I was focused on the natural beauty around me—and not looking for song ideas. I get ideas all the time from movies, books, conversations, and from other songs. It's rare for me to read a good book, look at a beautiful painting, or attend a great concert without my own creativity being sparked. The key is to keep the channel open, to look for those ideas that are all around us, and then to tell that internal critic to show a little respect and be quiet because there's an artist at work.

ARTISTIC IDENTITY

Last night I watched a performance by a terrific singer who is hoping to land a recording contract. Her voice is one of the best I've ever heard and she seemed perfectly in command of the stage, holding the audience in the palm of her hand. She effortlessly changed her style from one song to the next, starting out with a down-home Country tune and following that with a Mariah Carey R&B song. Throughout the show she included a Jazz standard, several original songs that might be at home on the current Pop charts, the B-52s' "Love Shack," and a Broadway belter from *Les Miz*' before ending with a rousing Gospel sing-along.

This woman obviously had no clue that versatility is a plus only if you're a demo session singer or looking for gigs singing at weddings, in nightclubs, or on cruise ships. But for a recording artist in search of a record deal, it's the kiss of death. Record labels and radio stations want to be able to pigeonhole their artists—and listeners want to be able to feel as though they "know" their favorite singers. It won't work if you present multiple, conflicting images to your audience.

It's crucial for a recording artist to develop and present a clearly defined identity. It is *not* effective for an aspiring recording artist to present a demo tape that features one Country song, one Pop number, and one Jazz tune. (However, if you are a songwriter who is writing for artists other than yourself, the ability to write successfully in a variety of styles can be a plus.) If you're capable of singing in several different styles, explore them thoroughly and make a decision about which one feels like the best "fit," taking into account your vocal capabilities as well as your personality and the image you'll be comfortable presenting.

Even an artist like Madonna, who's built an incredible career by continuously developing and transforming herself, maintains a clear thread that runs through her various incarnations. The audience needs to believe that the persona being presented to them is real in order for a performance to be effective. Maybe that's why the Garth Brooks' alter ego Chris Gaines' Pop project failed to garner a large audience. Fans were uncomfortable accepting that the star they love was not a "real person," but a calculated, carefully crafted image.

The audience needs to believe that Britney Spears is indeed the sexy tease she portrays; that Reba McEntire is broken hearted when she sings a sad song; and that the gangsta rapper is really a hardcore street thug. Even if it's an illusion, it's one that the audience wants maintained.

If I ask you to think about Tina Turner, you get a crystal clear image of the strong, sexy survivor. Likewise, if I ask you to describe Marie Osmond, some of the adjectives you might come up with are "wholesome," "All-American," and "sweet." The reality is probably that there is much more to these women than the personas they choose to present on recordings and onstage.

It's likely that Tina Turner also has a soft, vulnerable, tender side. But expressing that aspect of herself would not be consistent with the image she portrays. Marie Osmond may indeed possess a wild, sexual side. But if she put on spike heels and sang Tina Turner's "Private Dancer" (in which the singer presents herself as a worker in the sex trade) it would be jarring, even laughable to her audience—because it would be totally incongruous with the way they've come to see and define her.

Why all this talk about artists' images? How does it affect us as songwriters? Songs are among the most important components that help define an artist's identity. For example, the seething rage and intensity of Alanis Morissette's "You Oughta Know" was a clear expression of the persona she chose to put forth. Prince's songs ooze the raw sexuality and passion that fans associate with that artist. The songs Shania Twain writes and records tell the world she's sexy, strong, independent, and not afraid to flaunt it.

When we pitch our songs to artists, we need to be sure that these songs are consistent with the image that the artist has chosen to project. When you have an opportunity to present songs for a particular artist, don't waste the listener's time with songs that may be good but are not geared to his or her act. An A&R person at a major record label once told me that few things make him angrier than when someone has failed to do his or her homework—and makes that clear by pitching songs that are totally inappropriate for a project.

I remember very early on in my career pitching a song to a producer for R&B/Pop stars Earth, Wind, and Fire. It was the best song I'd ever written at the time, and I convinced myself that the producer would recognize this and record it with the band—in spite of the fact that, stylistically, this particular song was not even in the ballpark. It was much better suited for an adult contemporary balladeer like Barry Manilow or Neil Diamond—and the producer's response made that clear.

The music business is built upon relationships. So make the most of every opportunity to pitch your songs by doing your homework so those doors will remain open the next time, and the time after that.

Exercise

Pick one of your songs. Think about an artist you would like to pitch it to. Then answer the following questions:

✓ Is your song (and demo) in the musical style that this artist records?

✓ Does the lyric project an image that's consistent with the one this artist portrays?

✓ Is the lyric appropriate for the artist's age?

✓ Is this a song that could take the artist to a "next level"?

Remember that artists typically do not want to repeat themselves. There's a difference between a song that's *consistent* with the kind of material an artist records—versus one rehashing the same lyrical themes and melodic motifs that the artist has already covered.

HOW DARE YOU SAY I CAN'T ACCEPT CRITICISM?

My publisher once stopped a cassette player after listening to the first verse and chorus of my latest masterpiece. He removed the cassette, threw it across his desk, and said, "If I wanted shit like this, I'd go stop some amateur on Music Row." Ouch!

Let's face it: no one wants to be told his work isn't good enough. My initial reaction was anger; I was angry with my publisher for failing to recognize and acknowledge my brilliance. I thought, "Don't you realize who I think I am?" The truth is that he had no vested interest in saying that my song wasn't good enough for him to take it to a pitch meeting with confidence that it would rise above the competition. Quite to the contrary; having signed me, it was in his best interest for me to become successful.

It took several hours, three phone calls to sympathetic friends, a hot bath, and a long walk before a new perspective began to take hold. I reminded myself that my publisher's criticism was not motivated by a personal vendetta against me. If he didn't believe in my talent he wouldn't have signed me, and he certainly wouldn't be devoting his time and energy pushing me to become the best writer I could be. As the person who brought me into this company, he could only benefit from my success; my hits would be a feather in his cap. In retrospect, while I would have preferred a bit more nurturing, I see it would have been far more cruel to tell me how "wonderful" my songs were, when they weren't—and to fail to push me to do my very best work.

Encouragement and emotional support are important for all of us, and maybe to an even greater extent for creative types. We artists are ultra-sensitive creatures. I slowly came to understand that it was my friends' and relatives' job to tell me that my songs were spectacular; that my songs were destined to become standards; that I was brilliant, extraordinarily talented, and an overall wonderful guy; and that there was surely a spot waiting for me in the Songwriters' Hall of Fame. My *publisher's* job was to give me the tools to become a successful professional.

I've critiqued songs professionally for more than ten years and have had only one bad experience being on the other side of the desk. In that instance, I was critiquing songs at a BMI (Broadcast Music International) Nashville Workshop and it was time to listen to the last song of the day. I often jokingly tell my students that they should volunteer to have their songs critiqued early in the session before I get cranky and rushed. But the truth is that it is easier for me to be gentle and encouraging when I'm not running behind schedule. As the day wears on, I'm more likely to cut to the chase, skip the nurturing, and focus directly on what needs to be fixed.

I listened to that final song of the day and, almost immediately, I could tell it would require some surgery. The song was basically good, although it had some serious flaws in the lyric, but nothing too tough to repair. When I gave my diagnosis to the writer, a kindly, white-haired grandfatherly type, I was stunned to have him respond to my suggestions with some very intense and inappropriate hostility.

My constructive criticism was met with verbal abuse, defensiveness, and anger. What's sad is that the song really was pretty good. With a few lyric changes it might have been a contender. Instead, in one fell swoop, this guy managed to burn any chance of being invited back to one of the few places where he could receive the help he needed to achieve what he wanted so badly.

Let's face it, every critiquer is not going to be dead on for every song he or she reviews. I once had a respected publisher tell me that no one would ever record "Change My Mind" unless I changed the title. I've had other professionals make suggestions that seemed equally ludicrous, and I'm sure I've made my share of mistakes while critiquing songs.

So, what's the most beneficial way to accept criticism—especially if you don't agree with it? Let the reviewer know that you appreciate his or her time and opinion, that you will seriously consider incorporating their suggestions. Then, in the privacy of your car, you can laugh hysterically all the way home. You can tell your friends about the idiot you met with and never ask his or her opinion again. But do it without burning the bridge that may lead to a future record company president's door. The music business is relatively small, and there are a limited number of doors we can walk through. Make sure they don't lock behind you when you leave.

If a critique resonates and you think, "Wow, why didn't I think of that?" then obviously you'll want to rewrite and incorporate the changes. But if you disagree, get some additional professional opinions. See if there's a consensus. If there is, a rewrite is probably in order. Remember, if you don't like your rewrite better than what you started with you can always revert to the original version. By rewriting, you just might be able to take a really good song and make it a hit song. What do you have to lose?

It still hurts me every time my publisher tears one of my songs apart. It really stings to be told that what we created and love isn't as good as we'd hoped. But I'd rather get squashed today, lick my wounds, and be phenomenally successful next year than think my songs are perfect and never get them recorded. Wouldn't it be heartbreaking if you let a little pride and ego get in the way of a dream coming true?

TWO HATS

In all the years that I've been teaching songwriting workshops, I've never heard a song-writer say that what he or she really loves most about songwriting is the business. I've yet to meet a writer who writes songs as a means to an end, because his or her true passion is typing cover letters, networking with music business professionals, soliciting publishers, making CD copies, negotiating contracts, and pitching to record labels. To the contrary, one of the most common complaints I hear is, "I just want to be creative and write songs. I hate the thought of having to promote myself and my work."

Creative people who earn a living from what they create—whether their medium is acting, painting, directing, singing, writing novels or screenplays, or any other creative endeavor—are those who find ways to market themselves. Writing can be a wonderful hobby and a fulfilling means of self-expression; you can get tremendous satisfaction from engaging in the creative process and sharing the results with your family and friends. But if your goal is to write songs that Celine Dion will record, it won't be enough simply to write potential hits and wait for her to knock on your door.

Music business attorneys don't need to be able to write hit songs, and record label executives don't need to be able to sing. But successful songwriters and other artists are required to wear two hats: one that sits on top of our creative, sensitive self, and another that sits atop the part of us that's required to be a salesman. Like it or not, if you choose songwriting as a profession, it involves aspects that you may not enjoy, like virtually any other job. I used to imagine that songwriters lounged by their swimming pools, sipping iced tea and waiting for a brilliant idea to strike them. Ha! The successful song-writers I know work long and hard on creating their songs—and on marketing them.

I remember when Diane Warren, the most successful songwriter of our time, had her office above mine at RCA Records in Hollywood. Diane would already be hard at work when I arrived early in the morning. Most of the time her car was still parked in the lot when I left in the evening. Many of those nights, she'd go to the recording studio to work on demos, putting in twelve- or fourteen-hour workdays. So much for lounging by the pool.

Prior to signing my staff-writing deal, much of my energy was spent pursuing a publisher. This entailed networking with other songwriters who had relationships with publishers, and showing up and schmoozing at music business events where publishers would be found. Long before I ever had a song on the charts, I was a member of ASCAP (the American Society of Composers, Authors, and Publishers) and found the annual membership meetings that I attended to be a treasure trove of industry contacts. Songwriter organizations such as ASCAP, BMI (Broadcast Music International), NSAI (Nashville Songwriters' Association International), SGA (Songwriters Guild of America), and Taxi sometimes sponsor events that offer opportunities to pitch songs directly to publishers.

I attended these events religiously, and, as a direct result, had quite a few meetings with music publishers, including the one that lead to my first publishing contract. Of course, if you do not live near a major music center, it's unlikely that these kinds of opportunities will be available to you. But if you're serious about pursuing songwriting as a career, you might want to plan visits to cities where such events take place.

Now that I'm signed to a publishing deal, part of my time is spent trying to persuade my pluggers that out of the thousands of songs in their catalog, mine are the ones they should be pitching today. Since I don't often successfully manage to convince them of this, another large chunk of my time is spent augmenting my publisher's song-plugging efforts. This includes investigating which artists are currently looking for songs, pitching my songs, and setting up meetings with record labels, artists, and managers. If I had to venture a guess, I'd estimate that at least half of my work time is spent on aspects of my career that would not typically be categorized as "creative" endeavors.

Remember that getting your songs heard by music business professionals is an important part of your job. It's likely that getting your foot in the door will not be easy, and there's no tried-and-true formula to follow. If you've decided that you want to pursue songwriting as a profession, accept that there is much more to the business than just writing songs. Instead of fighting that fact, embrace it. You may even find that you enjoy the business.

I WANT IT NOW-OW-OW

I adored my Aunt Syb. She had no children of her own and treated me as if I were a prince. I could do no wrong through her eyes. I've often felt this world would be a much better place if everyone had their very own Aunt Syb—someone who believed in them totally and loved them completely and unconditionally.

When I was three or four years old, I would sometimes spend weekends with my aunt and her husband, my Uncle Mooney. She'd say, "We'll have good fun together," and we did! We would eat Velveeta cheese and go to the Cherry Hill Mall and buy things to make crafts projects. Making fried marbles was my favorite. We'd look at old family pictures and she'd tell me stories about the strange-looking people in those photographs who lived in foreign countries, but were somehow connected to me.

Through her eyes I was the smartest, best-looking, most-talented, perfect child. But from what I've heard from other sources in my family I was not exactly the easiest kid to deal with. I was stubborn, prone to tantrums, and fiercely impatient. When I couldn't get my way I would stamp my feet, clench my fists, and with all the resolve and fury that only a three-year-old can possess I'd shout, "I want it and I want it now-ow-ow-ow-ow!!!"

As I grew older, the bond I shared with my Aunt Syb grew stronger and stronger. She and my Uncle Moon are gone now, but throughout my life they'd sometimes tease me and mimic little three-year old Jason stamping his feet and demanding, "I want it now-ow-ow!"

That three-year-old still lives somewhere inside me. Some days he lives closer to the surface than others, but he'll probably always be a part of me. He wants immediate gratification, and doesn't deal well with having to wait. In fact, he's been known to say, "I want it and I want it now. No, now is too late because I've already waited too long!" When he writes a song he wants it to be the Number One smash hit on the radio the next day.

I'm the kind of person who plants a seed and then stands over it waiting for it to sprout. I've also been known to tap my foot and stand with my arms crossed, snarling at the microwave, "Hurry up, I don't have all *minute*." No, patience is definitely not something I was blessed with.

No matter how frustrating it is, the immutable reality is that all I can do is plant my seed in the proper soil, feed and water it, place it in a sunny spot conducive to its growth—and wait. I can stamp my feet, demand that it grow, and curse it for taking so long, but Mother Nature will still take her course on her own timetable.

Waiting is one of the toughest things for me to do, but the only other choice is to rail against it, get frustrated, complain—and still get the same results. No matter how much I wish it were not true, some seeds take a very long time to germinate, and others are not meant to bring forth flowers.

When I moved to Los Angeles, I *knew* I'd become a rich and famous singer/songwriter within a year. But that's not how it happened. As the years went by without fame or fortune knocking at my door, I became convinced that if only I didn't have to work a day job, then I would become rich and famous within a year. But I did need to support myself as almost all struggling actors, songwriters, musicians, writers, and artists do. It took eleven-and-a-half years before I signed a staff-writing deal.

My first summer in Nashville was sweltering and the attic I rented was neither well insulated nor air conditioned. I remember it being so hot that I was afraid I would die. No one knew it, but sometimes I would go to my publisher's air-conditioned office to sleep on the weekends. So much for instantly becoming a rich and famous songwriter.

The bottom line is that success in the music business rarely happens quickly. For every story of overnight success, there are probably a hundred stories of writers and artists who invested years and years before achieving their goals. For example, "I Swear," (written by Gary Baker and Frank J. Myers) spent an incredible fifteen weeks at Number One (between *Billboard's* Pop and Country charts) and in the 1990s was named the most performed song of the decade—after laying on a shelf for more than five years.

In retrospect I'm grateful for those years before I could earn a living as a songwriter; they gave me a chance to learn my craft and learn about myself before being thrust into the competition. But after all these years I still want to get to that next level of success, and there's a three-year-old inside me stamping his feet and screaming, "I want it now-ow-ow!"

CAREER SINGLES

Before Britney Spears soared to the top of the charts with "...Baby One More Time" we had never heard anything quite like it on the radio. Swedish writer/producer Max Martin carved out an identity for Britney and secured her place in the annals of Pop music when he wrote that song. I'm not sure we'd know who Britney Spears is if there had never been a "...Baby One More Time."

The songs that establish an artist or take that artist to the next level of success are known as "career singles." A prime example is "This Kiss," the song that transformed Faith Hill from a moderately successful Country act to a bona fide crossover superstar. Similarly, "I Try" was a springboard to jumpstart Macy Gray's career, as was "The Dance" for Garth Brooks, "I'm Like a Bird" for Nelly Furtado, and "Complicated" for Avril Lavigne. And where would Train be without "Drops of Jupiter?" Think about the single song you most strongly identify with each of your favorite artists. I bet you'll agree that in each of these songs the lyrics and the melodies were exciting, daring, and, most importantly, something we'd never heard before.

There are hundreds of additional examples of songs that were responsible for propelling artists (and writers) to heights they'd only dreamed of. I suspect that in her wildest dreams, traditional Country singer Lee Ann Womack never imagined she'd be riding the top of the Country *and* Pop charts. "I Hope You Dance" was the vehicle that took her there. When writers Mark D. Sanders and Tia Sillers wrote that song it was fresh; it touched millions of hearts with a message that had never previously been expressed quite that way, either melodically or lyrically.

The writers took a chance the day they wrote that song. Instead of following the safe and easy path of chasing the hits on the radio, they blazed their own trail, as every innovator has. They created something truly special instead of another "good" song. That's what it takes to make a true impact in such a competitive arena. (By the way, this phenomenal song was rejected by several major artists before being recorded.)

Perfectly crafted songs won't cut it. There are probably more than a thousand professional staff-writers with major credits and connections who can crank out a perfectly crafted song five days a week. So how can you possibly beat out competition at that level? By writing songs that are distinctive, original, and creative—not just good.

Writing about this reminds me of an experience I had a few years ago when I went to New York to meet with A&R representatives at various record labels to play songs for their artists. Every person I met with thought my songs were good (which they were), but they didn't get excited enough to put them on hold for their projects. At several of the meetings, when I asked what they were looking for, I was told, "Bring me an 'Unbreak My Heart.'" At the time, Toni Braxton's recording of Diane Warren's "Unbreak My Heart" had recently been at the top of the Pop, Adult Contemporary, and R&B charts.

So what did they mean when they requested another "Unbreak My Heart?" Surely they didn't want another song that sounded just like that one. We already had one. Did they mean they wanted a song with Spanish guitars; a melody that begins low and jumps up an octave; a title that includes a word the writer made up? Were they asking for a song with that tempo and groove; a chorus with an unexpected modulation; a lyric about a woman who wishes her lover would return? I don't think so. I suspect that these record executives were actually trying to say, "We need a great song that's fresh, original, and unique."

We've heard the concept, "You hurt me and I wish you'd come back and love me again," a thousand times. But Diane Warren found a way to approach this topic in a totally new way, both melodically and lyrically. That's why it was special. I think the A&R representatives I met with were really asking for songs that would break new ground; songs that would push the creative envelope, and somehow separate themselves from the countless hundreds of other perfectly crafted, really good songs they screen day in and day out.

When they initially exploded onto the music scene, artists such as Alicia Keyes, Linkin Park, and the Dixie Chicks weren't following trends. Artists like these create the trends. That's what we need to do as writers. Be an innovator. Be a trailblazer. It's our job as writers to stay ahead of the curve and give tomorrow's superstars the songs that will help create their distinctive sounds.

The next time you watch a televised music awards show (e.g., the Grammys), take note of how unique and fresh those songs that get nominated for top honors are. Nobody earns an award or makes it to the top of the charts by following trends or by rehashing ideas that have already been successful.

Write the kind of songs that set the standard; the songs that other writers try to emulate and wish they had written. If you hope to make a real impact, probably the most dangerous thing you can do is to play it safe.

Exercise

Analyze a favorite song that was an artist's first hit. Write down the lyrics. If you're a musician, figure out how to play the song. Then answer the following questions:

- ✓ What is special and unique about the lyric?
- ✓ Did the writer(s) find a new angle, a new way to express his or her idea?
- ✓ What is it about the melody and rhythm that sets this song apart?

HOLD THIS

I had a pretty good meeting this morning. I pitched songs to Tiffany Swinea at Gallimore Productions, the company responsible for producing artists including Faith Hill, Tim McGraw, Jessica Andrews, and Jo Dee Messina. I played portions of fifteen songs—which is about twice as many as I would normally play at a pitch meeting. But Tiffany knew what she was looking for, and if she didn't hear it, she'd move on to the next song after listening to the first chorus.

At the end of the meeting she'd asked to hold onto copies of five songs. So does that mean I had five songs "on hold?" No. This is a common misconception that I want to clear up. There's a world of difference between holding onto songs, and placing a song "on hold."

A "hold" is an agreement whereby a songwriter or publisher grants the listener the exclusive right for his or her recording artist to be the first one to record a particular song. When a writer or publisher agrees to give a hold, he or she is essentially saying, "If you choose to record this song I promise that you can be the first artist to release it. If I play it for anyone else, I'll let them know that it is already on hold, and won't let any other artist record it until you've either released your version—or decided not to record the song."

A hold is typically a verbal agreement, and it's rare that any paperwork is exchanged. Reba McEntire is among those very few artists who sometimes sends a letter of confirmation when she has placed a song on hold. I've received two of those letters, as well as a phone message requesting a hold from Ms. McEntire—but no Reba cuts so far.

Who places songs on hold? A&R representatives at record labels, producers, managers, and, in some instances, the artists themselves. Of course, the more people in decision-making positions who have heard the song, the better the shot and the "stronger" the hold. Until the artist and producer have heard the song, there are still some important hoops for it to get through.

The first time I had a song go on hold was in 1990, when my cowriter A.J. Masters' publisher Bull's Creek Music played "Change My Mind" directly to the Oak Ridge Boys. The Oaks loved the song and asked for a hold until they were scheduled to begin recording their next album—five months later.

In the interim, another artist, Robin Lee, who'd had a recent hit with the country version of "Black Velvet," wanted to record the song. But after confirming that the Oak Ridge Boys, who had it on hold, still intended to record the song, we had to tell Robin that she could not have the song. Bear in mind that we ran the risk of losing the cut with Robin Lee—and having the Oak Ridge Boys decide not to record the song. It was also possible that the Oaks could have recorded the song, but decided not to release it. These were chances we were willing to take in order to maintain our credibility and working relationship with a superstar act.

There are instances when a publisher or writer decides not to honor a hold and gives the song to another artist, especially if the second artist is more successful than the one who originally requested the hold. But the music business is small and it's not a good idea to make enemies.

Ironically, years later Robin Lee (who went on to become a wonderful, successful songwriter) and I became friends and collaborators. She confided in me that she had already recorded the song when she was denied the right to release it. She said that when she later toured with the Oak Ridge Boys, she stood crying on the side of the stage when they performed what she felt would have been a big hit for her. But she understood and respected our decision to deny her the opportunity to release the song first.

The Oak Ridge Boys did record my song. But far more often than not, holds do not develop into cuts—just disappointments. The artist, record label, and producer typically have many more songs on hold than they could possibly record. Some artists and their representatives may place more than two hundred songs on hold for an album that will include only eleven. As it gets closer to the time when the album will be recorded, some of the songs that are on hold are dropped, and replaced by others.

Timing is important when it comes to pitching songs. It's not a good idea to pitch a song when an artist may be a year or more away from recording. Even if they fall in love with your song, you run the risk of their tiring of it, or of being "bumped" when a fresh, new song comes along at the last minute. Also, in the event that a given artist requests a hold on your song long before he or she is ready to record, you are effectively eliminating additional (possibly better) opportunities to pitch your song that might come along in the interim.

Writers are not paid, or compensated in any other way, for granting a hold, and by doing so may tie up their songs, miss other opportunities to get the songs cut, and, ultimately, not get the songs recorded at all. The artist, or his or her representatives, have nothing to lose by holding as many songs as they choose for as long as they want.

It sounds like a raw deal for the writers and publishers, so you might ask, "Why grant holds?" The answer is that for now, it's simply the way business is done. If you refuse to grant a hold, the artist might choose a different song. Here's a scenario to ponder: if Jennifer Lopez said she was planning to record her next album in six months and was seriously considering recording your song—but was holding fifty additional songs— would you be willing to tie up your song for all that time? You can bet that I would.

Once you've granted a hold, it's important to maintain contact with the person who requested it, and try to get answers in a reasonable amount of time. You won't always be accommodated, but, for example, you might ask if they would be willing to request a response from the producer and artist within the next four weeks.

Of course, even if all the decision makers agree that they like the song and want to keep it on hold, there's no guarantee that it will be recorded. But at least you'll know that it's a serious contender. If someone in the chain decides he doesn't like the song, the hold is released, and you are now free to lick your wounds and begin pitching the song to other artists.

When my first hold turned into a cut, I had no idea how lucky I was. I didn't have such good luck with my second hold. The moment "What Would Happen" was put on hold for Country star Lorrie Morgan, I began calculating how much money I would make. In the six months that elapsed between when the song was placed on hold and when Lorrie was scheduled to record, I heard rumors about how much Lorrie loved the song. I even received a note saying that the head of her record label thought it would be a huge single for her.

Each rumor added fuel to the fire of my imagination, which was already working overtime. By the time someone told me he'd heard the demo of my song playing at Lorrie's manager's office (where everyone agreed it would be a hit), I'd begun meeting with realtors and looking at new cars. (I'm not kidding.)

I knew which days Lorrie was scheduled to be recording her album and I compulsively checked my phone messages at least twenty times a day waiting to receive the good news. I was a basket case by the end of that week, when I still hadn't heard anything. You can imagine how devastated I was when I learned that they'd attempted to record the song, and quickly decided that it wasn't right for Lorrie. I think this song must be cursed. It's been on hold seventeen times, was recorded three times, and has never been released.

Since then I've had more than a hundred holds. There was one year when I had nearly thirty songs on hold—and got only two recorded. Neither one became a hit. I've had songs fail to get recorded after being on hold for more than six months. I had one situation where the artist and producer swore to my publisher that they were going to record the song "on the fifteenth," and didn't.

In one instance, I was told an artist "loved" my song. When I met him at a party it was obvious that he'd never heard it. I once had an artist take a copy of my song out of her purse and gush that she and her secretary loved the song so much that it made them cry. She didn't record it.

I've learned from painful experience that a hold does not mean that I'm about to get a cut. But it's definitely a step in the right direction. Now I take the news of a hold as confirmation that my song is indeed as strong as I'd hoped, and that it's a contender: nothing more, nothing less. I still get excited when I get holds. I just don't allow myself to count on them turning into cuts.

The good news is that I don't get nearly as devastated anymore when I lose a hold. I used to get depressed for a month. Now it lasts twenty minutes.

FROM THE HEART—AND FOR THE RADIO

When I moved to Los Angeles in 1979, I left behind a relationship, a career, and my family in order to be closer to my dream. I wanted a hit song as much as I've ever wanted anything in my life. But I was like a hamster on a wheel. When it came to my songwriting, I kept doing the same thing over and over again and not understanding why I wasn't getting different results.

I wrote songs that were deeply personal expressions of my angst. They didn't conform to any structure, didn't include melodic repetition or choruses, and didn't necessarily include the title within the song. But it never occurred to me that I was not writing the kinds of songs that would likely help me to fulfill my dreams. Honestly, I thought the only reason my songs weren't on the radio was because I didn't have the right connections and hadn't yet gotten that elusive lucky break.

I hadn't yet learned to master the skills necessary to write songs that were geared toward the commercial radio market. While that was certainly a big stumbling block, probably the biggest problem was that I was writing from my heart—with zero consideration for the listeners. I assumed that if my song had an emotional impact on me, it would have a similar effect upon millions of anonymous listeners in Radioland. But it doesn't necessarily work that way.

I knew exactly what my words intended. No one else did. My subtle and often intentionally obtuse lyrics made perfect sense to me, but anyone outside of my immediate circle of friends didn't stand a chance of understanding *or feeling* what I had intended. This would have been fine if my intention was to write strictly for my own enjoyment, but it wasn't.

I was writing solely as a means of self-expression—to please myself. It never even occurred to me to attempt to include my listeners in the equation. But effective songwriting doesn't just please the writer. The audience should feel as though the song speaks to them and touches their hearts. This doesn't happen by coincidence, but by expressing yourself in such a way that the melody and lyric successfully evokes the desired feeling in your listeners.

Writing from your heart is crucial. Why bother if your idea isn't important to you? If you're trying to manufacture something that's not real for you, it's unlikely that you'll be able to do it as well or better than someone for whom it is. I needed to learn how to take those ideas that began as a spark in my heart and to package them and express them in ways that would touch other hearts.

Writing from your heart and expressing it in a manner that can connect with millions of listeners does not have to be mutually exclusive. Nor does it have to be equated with selling out. You don't necessarily need to change the essence of your song or its message in order to accomplish successful communication. But you might need to incorporate tried-and-true techniques and tools that will help you deliver your message to your listeners.

Commercial potential is certainly not the only way to judge the value of a song, but *if* your intent is to achieve commercial success (and it doesn't have to be), you need to write songs that successfully communicate. The first step is becoming aware that the goal is to move beyond the stage of writing for ourselves. Then we can begin learning to consciously express our ideas in ways that will stand the best chance of reaching our intended audience.

Once I realized what I needed to do in order to achieve success, I began working on acquiring and practicing the skills, tools, and techniques that would deliver my songs from my heart to my listeners. It wasn't a quick or easy journey, but at least I was on my way.

You can certainly write solely for your own satisfaction. That's a perfectly viable option. But don't write songs that fail to take your audience into consideration, and then be angry and frustrated because no one records or publishes them.

Exercise

Write down the titles of several of your original songs. Take a good hard look and try to be as objective as possible when answering the following questions:

- ✓ If you do not plan to record these songs yourself, are they appropriate for artists who do not write their own material?

- ✓ Are you taking the commercial marketplace into consideration—or writing exclusively for yourself?

Now make a list of artists for whom each of your songs would be well suited. If you refer to current singles charts you'll get lots of pitch ideas. You'll also be able to see which artists record material that they (or their producers) did not write.

BRIDGE ME

My friend Hunter Davis and I recently had a cowriting session to rewrite the lyric for a melody we had begun a few days earlier. The previous couple of times I had worked on songs I wasn't satisfied with any of my ideas. I felt like I was trying to force them, and the harder I tried, the more contrived and trite my lyrics seemed. I was frustrated and irritated with myself.

Before leaving for my writing session I headed to the garden for my favorite therapy. As I weeded, puttered, and watered, my focus was on the herbs, flowers, and vegetables, not on writing songs. My lousy mood faded as I looked for new buds and pruned away old growth. I soon found myself humming the melody that Hunter and I had written. Before I knew it, a lyric was pouring out of me and it was good—*really* good.

When I arrived at Hunter's house I announced, "I've got great news. Our lyric's finished, except for the bridge." She looked at me and said, "You *bridged* me. I can't believe you bridged me!" I had never heard that expression and asked her what she meant. She laughed and said that the expression describes a situation where a writer brings a collaborator a completely finished lyric, or even an entire song—except for the bridge. She explained that it's a tactic some writers use when they're writing with a major artist who may not be a very good writer, but wants to contribute to the songs.

Hunter's a wonderful writer with hits under her belt, and she's more than capable of writing great songs. I wasn't trying to edge her out of the creative process; I was just on a roll. Sometimes, one collaborator contributes more than the other, while at other times the other writer may be the one who comes up with the magic line that makes the song a hit. It's not productive to count who wrote which words and melody lines. Unless some other agreement is decided upon in advance, if there are two writers, it's understood that the split will be fifty–fifty. But this situation with Hunter brought up an interesting issue: How much is too much to bring to a collaboration?

When I wrote "Change My Mind," I brought in a completely finished lyric, except for the bridge. That was my first Nashville cowriting session and I was a nervous wreck, so I wanted to be sure that I would successfully contribute during the meeting. I've done that on several occasions since, especially when it's a "high-pressure" writing situation (i.e., with a major artist or a high-profile writer.)

I've been on the receiving end of being "bridged." In a couple of instances, I was asked by students to collaborate on songs that seemed to be completely finished. It was obvious that the main thing these would-be collaborators hoped I would add to their songs was my name at the bottom of the lyric sheets. I was insulted that they thought I would want to work that way. However, while it's not a common occurrence, I have heard of situations where well-known recording artists do just that.

In one instance, I "wrote" with a very successful artist who sat reading magazines while I did all the work. I ran lyrics and melodies past him to see if he liked them, but it was evident he was more interested in being listed as a writer than in actually writing the song. But most of the artists I've worked with tried their best to contribute, even if they were not experienced writers.

I know a couple of very successful songwriters who are so trusting of their instincts that they do not typically bring any ideas to a writing session. They're incredible writers and they've learned to trust that they will come up with something. Their process seems to work for them. But most professional writers maintain a file of potential song titles, lyric phrases, images, and/or melodic snippets that they present to cowriters. Personally, I do my best work when I do my homework, but I always remain open to my partner's input, using whatever I've brought to the collaboration simply as a starting place.

THE VIEW FROM THE OTHER SIDE OF THE DESK

Since I spent more than five years paying my rent by working for RCA Records in Los Angeles, I'm often asked how someone can get a job at a record label or music publishing company. I got that job by being sent out as a "temp" from an agency that specialized in providing temporary employees to the entertainment industry. I figured that if I had to temp, I might as well learn about the music business and make some connections.

I got to know many of the RCA department heads, and when a full-time position opened up, I was someone whose work they already knew and trusted. Like me, many of the people who got hired for those coveted jobs at RCA and other record labels started either as temps or as interns from a college. Ten years later, some of those temps and interns are now in high-level positions in the industry.

Part of my time at RCA was spent in the A&R (Artists and Repertoires) department—the "creative" department that signs artists to the label, oversees their development, and helps find songs for those acts that don't write their own. My responsibilities included screening the songs pitched for our artists, including Starship, the Pointer Sisters, Diana Ross, and Barry Manilow, as well as for Country stars such as the Judds, Kenny Rogers, Dolly Parton, and Alabama.

Years later, to supplement my income during my first years as a staff-writer, my record label experience helped me land a part-time job as production coordinator for producer/studio musician extraordinaire Steve Gibson. At this job my primary duties were administrative: handling budgets, booking musicians and recording studios, screening phone calls, compiling label copy (the writer and publisher information that is printed on an album and its insert), as well as general typing and filing. But I also helped review the songs that were pitched for the hit Country albums Steve produced, which included Randy Travis, McBride and the Ride, and Aaron Tippin.

At times it felt like torture to be working with so many successful writers and artists. I was close enough to my dreams to almost reach out and touch them, yet I was behind the desk listening to *other* writers' songs, not having my own songs recorded. Nonetheless, I learned some incredibly valuable lessons about what it's like to sit on the "other" side of the desk.

The publishers, A&R representatives, producers, and other industry pros you meet with are in business to make money—not to teach you how to write songs. Expecting a publisher to be able to articulate why she hasn't selected your song is like going on a job interview with two hundred other equally qualified applicants and expecting a detailed explanation of why another applicant was chosen. You may be well qualified, but they just liked the other person better.

When a publisher, producer, or record company executive says, "No" to your song, the chances are good that he or she doesn't know why it doesn't sound like a hit. She may be skilled at recognizing a potential hit, but that's a very different talent from being able to verbalize how to turn a good song into a hit song. Sometimes it's not possible. There are lots of perfectly crafted songs that have nothing wrong with them; they simply aren't special enough to edge out the competition. They may not have a particularly fresh lyrical angle, or maybe the melody isn't "Wow."

Some publishers (especially those who began their careers as songwriters) are highly adept at critiquing songs, but, sadly, they are definitely in the minority. Even if they know what's missing in your song (and they probably don't), unless you're signed as a staffwriter to their company it's not their responsibility to invest their valuable time in teaching you. If you remember that publishers and other industry professionals are in business and are required to produce results in order to keep their jobs, it may be easier to avoid taking it personally if they are unwilling to meet with you or spend much time with you in the event that you do get a meeting. Remember that meeting with new writers is only one part of their job, and they get dozens of meeting requests per week.

Similarly, many developing writers seem to think that professional songwriters should be willing to critique their material, cowrite with them, and introduce them to publishers. We wouldn't expect that of a professional in any other industry. Can you imagine picking an attorney's name out of the phone book and cold calling, saying, "I'm studying for the Bar Exam. Would you be willing to explain paragraph three in Chapter five and give me some other advice? Oh, and then will you introduce me to your boss because I'm looking for a job?"

It seems ludicrous, yet I regularly receive lyrics or songs mailed to me from total strangers in every corner of the world who expect just that kind of input. It would be wonderful if this world worked that way, but we all have responsibilities and a limited amount of time in which to accomplish them. I give back as much as I can to the songwriting community by teaching workshops, writing books and articles, and producing instructional CDs. But I've had to learn to erect and maintain boundaries, or I would expend so much energy helping other songwriters that I wouldn't have a career.

Back when I worked in the A&R department at RCA I coined the phrase "A&R'mor" (get it? Armor!) to describe those boundaries that I had to maintain to survive in a position where it felt as though everyone in the world wanted to buy me lunch and take a piece of me home with them.

The people we want to get our songs to (i.e., top producers and A&R reps) are bombarded with submissions, often more than 100 CDs per day. More than they have time to listen to come from a handful of the most successful writers and publishers with whom they have personal relationships. Put yourself in their shoes. If they have an extra hour (which they don't), would their time be best spent meeting with and listening to songs by writers who have not yet established a track record? Or might they have a better shot of finding that smash hit single by having lunch with Diane Warren's rep or meeting with Keith Follese's (*Billboard* Country Writer of the Year), Desmond Child's, Babyface's, or Ja Rule's representatives?

From their point of view, it's nothing personal. You've either got what they need, or their time is better spent elsewhere. Time is money, and those who keep their jobs and move ahead in the highly competitive music business know they have to use their time wisely. They're deluged daily with writers who have varying degrees of talent and are at varying stages in their development. They don't owe them an education. Only those writers in the top one percent are of any interest to the legit pro.

Am I saying that it's hopeless and that you should give up? Of course not. I am saying not to take rejection personally. Imagine the other person's perspective. The music business can seem cold and hard—because sometimes it is! It's fiercely competitive, and rejection, disappointment, and frustration are all parts of the package. Be ready to deal with them. (And they're going to hurt more than you expect, no matter how well you try to prepare yourself.)

I understand how frustrating this perspective is for a writer who doesn't have a track record yet. I was in that category for many years. I know that it can feel like a Catch-22; like you can't get there from here. But, every writer who is currently successful started out with dreams—not hits. Success requires exceptional songs and hard work (peppered with a dash of luck) on both the creative *and* business sides.

Give the person behind the desk a reason to want to meet with you. Study and practice your craft. Become one of those writers whom the industry pros can count on to bring them hits consistently. In the meantime, don't take it personally when they don't want to teach you how to improve your songs. That's not their job, and they probably don't know how—or they'd be writing hit songs.

HOW TO GET A STAFF-WRITING DEAL

Getting a staff-writing deal is simple. All you need to do is get a song recorded by a major-label recording artist with a track record and offer publishers the right to publish your song in exchange for a staff-writing deal. I guarantee you'll get offers. If you know your song will be a single, you'll get even better offers. Isn't that easy?

That really is how it worked for me. In 1991, nearly a dozen years after I'd moved to Los Angeles, my writing had progressed tremendously. I'd had one song recorded on a tiny independent record label, but the royalties it generated were barely enough to celebrate at McDonald's, and I was still working at a day job.

As you learned in the "Staff-writing" chapter, a few years earlier I had taken my first trip to Nashville, and during that visit cowrote "Change My Mind." I was sure it would instantly be recorded by a superstar act. Three-and-a-half years and more than seventy-five rejections later, the Oak Ridge Boys recorded it. The Oaks were enormously successful artists at this point and our song was set to be their next single, following up a Number One hit for them.

Since I owned my share of the publishing, I had a huge decision to make. Should I hold onto my publishing, or sign it over as part of a deal with a publisher? If I kept my publishing, in the likely event that the song became a Top-Five single, as my own publisher I'd probably earn close to $100,000, in addition to the $100,000 I'd earn as the writer. But if I were willing to bring my publishing to the table, I could secure that staff-writing deal that I wanted so desperately.

I met with six Nashville publishing companies and was offered six deals for varying amounts of money, but none of them were even in the ballpark of the $100,000 I could potentially earn if I held onto my publishing—presuming my song became a hit (and *of course* it would). But then again, in the unlikely event that the song failed I'd have nothing—no money and no staff-writing deal.

One of the companies I met with, Zomba, offered me $5,000 less than one of the larger companies. Five thousand dollars was an enormous amount of money to me at that point in time. But I reminded myself that the money up front was simply an advance against my own future mechanical (sales) royalties and shouldn't be the sole factor in making such an important decision.

The publishers I met with at the other companies were very complimentary about my songs. The head of Zomba's Nashville office tore my songs to shreds, but he made them stronger—and taught me valuable lessons in the process. An added plus was that Zomba owned Jive Records, a very successful label, so I guessed I would have an inside edge to get my songs recorded. I had a strong sense that by working with Zomba I'd have the best shot at the career I'd always dreamed of. My decision was made.

When that Oak Ridge Boys' single peaked at #70 on the *Billboard* chart and then fizzled off, I was devastated. I couldn't have imagined it back then, but that song accomplished more for me than I could have dreamed of. When I decided I'd rather be a staff-writer than keep hold of my publishing, I could never have anticipated the chain of events that was being set in motion. Not only have I been able to earn a living as a songwriter ever since, but my songs landed on three of the best-selling albums of all time.

I didn't have a crystal ball and couldn't foresee the future. So I carefully examined all my options, determined my priorities, consulted experienced people I trusted (including an entertainment attorney), said a prayer, took a deep breath—and jumped. I landed where I'd always hoped to fall. Zomba believed in my talent, and developed and supported me for more than five years before I had hits. That's unheard of in this day and age.

If I had accepted one of the other, higher-paying offers, I would likely have had one or two years as staff-writer and then gone back home with my tail between my legs, because, although I didn't know it at the time, I needed more time to learn my craft. If I had held onto my publishing I would have had one hundred percent of nothing.

So I wasn't joking when I stated that the easiest way to secure a staff-writing deal is to bring a song to the table that has already been recorded by a major artist. Every writer doesn't have that opportunity, though. How do you get a staff-writing deal if you don't have a major track record and you don't own the publishing on an upcoming major release? There's no easy, cut-and-dried answer. But when it gets discouraging (and it will), remind yourself that every person currently earning a living as a staff-writer started out with a dream.

You've got to learn how to write exceptional songs: songs that publishers believe they can place with successful artists; songs that are unique, fresh, and special. Often, more than 1,200 songs are pitched by professional writers for a major artist's project. This means that if there are twelve slots on the album, presuming that the artist and producer don't write them (and they typically *will* write some of them), only the top one-tenth of one percent of the songs that are pitched will be included on the album. So you can see that it's tough for a publisher to secure a major cut for one of their writers. It's much easier for publishers if their writers are "inside" the projects—meaning the writer is also the artist or the producer, or has close ties with these individuals.

Many publishers sign singer/songwriters if they believe strongly in their talent. Then they get involved in the process of shopping a record deal. If they secure a recording contract for their artist, the publishing company will presumably publish many, if not all of the songs on the resulting album. Likewise, if a publishing company signs a writer who is also a record producer they are greatly increasing their chances of getting cuts with this writer.

Most staff-writers are instrumental in getting many of their own songs recorded. Demonstrating that you are well connected in the business, or able to contribute to the publisher's efforts, will make you a much more desirable prospect.

In the event that you are simply a songwriter (as opposed to a singer/songwriter or producer/songwriter), it should be clear why your songs need to be exceptional. If your songs still need work to edge out the competition, do whatever you need to do to get them to that next level. Study your craft, attend workshops, do songwriting exercises, and be willing to take risks and push the creative envelope with your writing.

But let's presume that your songs are incredible; now what? There are no easy answers. You can't earn a degree in songwriting and then send a resume to apply for a staff-writing deal. You've got to write great songs, demo them to present them in their best light, and then network, network, and network. (I know you don't want to hear this again.)

It's incredibly rare for a writer without a track record to simply schedule a meeting with a publisher, play some songs, and get offered a staff-writing deal on the spot. This is a huge commitment both financially and in terms of energy on the part of both parties, and it's not something that is entered into lightly. Like any relationship, the connection typically takes time to develop.

It starts with a publisher hearing songs he or she believes can get recorded. So, once you've got the songs, you've got to figure out ways to meet with publishers. Here are some suggestions:

- Attend songwriting and music business workshops.
- Interact and/or cowrite with writers who are meeting with publishers.
- Meet with reps from the performing rights societies (ASCAP, BMI, and SESAC in the U.S.).
- Join and become actively involved in songwriter organizations (e.g., NSAI, SGA, Taxi, or your local songwriting group).

- Make trips to songwriting centers (i.e., L.A., New York, or Nashville)

If you take these actions, *and have great songs*, the chances are good that you will find a publisher. In other words, once you've got potential hits it all comes down to taking care of business. As I've said earlier, this is just as important a part of your job as writing hits.

When you meet with a publisher, it's not realistic for a developing writer to expect to play a few songs and get offered a staff-writing deal. Unless you've brought in "This Kiss," "I Hope You Dance," "It's Hot in Heere," and "I'm Already There," it's probably not going to happen. A worthy goal for the initial meeting is to make a good enough impression to whet the publisher's appetite, so that you get invited back. Once you get a publisher's attention, he or she may set you up with several other writers and evaluate the results. Your work ethic, personality, and extent to which you're contributing to getting your own songs recorded will be assessed. A few of your songs may be signed to *Single Song Agreements*, or be pitched with the understanding that you will give the publisher all or some of your share of the publishing rights and royalties in the event that they secure a cut.

With luck, some of your songs will garner interest when the publisher plays them for artists, producers, and record label executives. The listeners will hopefully be enthusiastic enough to request copies of your songs. Some of them may go "on hold," and eventually be recorded.

When enough time has passed for you and the publisher to feel comfortable working together, if your songs are beginning to get some interest, and if you've targeted a company that signs staff-writers and is currently looking to add to its roster, it will probably be time to discuss a deal.

The scenarios I've described are ways that writers typically get signed to staff-writing deals. But just as there are no hard and fast rules in songwriting, there are no rules about how to achieve success on the business side of the music business; you may find other routes that lead you to success. I can't promise that everyone who wants to earn a living as a songwriter will have the same luck and opportunities that I had. But I do believe that writing great songs is not a matter of luck or chance. There are tools and techniques that can be mastered. If you do everything in your power to hone your skills, *and take care of business*, you'll have a great shot.

BE WHO YOU ARE

When I contracted to write *6 Steps to Songwriting Success: The Comprehensive Guide to Writing and Marketing Hit Songs* for Billboard Books, I had no idea how much work waited ahead of me. If I'd had any clue of how long it would take to finish one page, I would never have agreed to write 320 of them. Sometimes, ignorance truly is bliss.

Each morning when I sat down at my computer, all I could write was the very next page. When I found that I needed additional technical knowledge to write that particular page, my first task for that day became learning about that topic by calling people who were better informed in this area, researching online, or reading a book. It's much less overwhelming to commit to writing two pages this morning than it is to writing three hundred this year. I can't predict or control what may happen in six months, but I can commit to writing two pages today.

"But I'm not good enough. I'm really a fraud, a fake, a charlatan. They'll all see that I'm dressed in the emperor's new clothes. Besides, what's so special about me? The odds of becoming successful are one in a million. So many writers are so much more talented than I am. Maybe I should just give up and get a real job."

Now that I've given the voices in my head a chance to share, I can continue. I suspect we all share those particular messages (or similar ones). To a certain extent, they're true. There are plenty of writers far more gifted than I am. But, none with my unique perspective and particular set of life experiences—and none with yours.

It sounds silly, but you're the very best "you" there is. You'll never write a Diane Warren song or a Stephen King novel—but they'll never write the way you're capable of writing because you *and only you* have your own way of perceiving the world and interpreting situations based on your genetics and past experiences.

Tell the voices in your head, "Thank you for sharing. I really appreciate your concern and your desire to protect me from failure and ridicule. But I can take it and I'd rather fail than never try." (By the way, this works with parents, spouses, and friends, too.)

John Grisham wrote his first novel while riding to work on the subway each morning. J.K. Rowling was a single mom receiving government assistance when she created Harry Potter, one page at a time in a coffee shop. They weren't multimillionaires or household names back then. These writers, and countless others who have carved out success in creative endeavors, were simply "regular people" with a goal. They found ways to express and market their unique artistic visions. So can you.

I finished writing 6 *Steps to Songwriting Success* by working from 6:00 a.m. till 9:00 a.m. most mornings before going off to my full-time job of writing and pitching songs. Some mornings I wrote one page. On days when I was super-productive I completed three or four pages. I'd never written a book before but, somehow, those pages added up and at the end of eighteen months it was finished.

My books don't contain ultimate truths about the writing process. They simply express the tools and lessons I've picked up along my journey, my personal experiences, and my own way of looking at things. That's what makes them special and different from other songwriting books.

Learn the tools that have repeatedly been used in successful songs. Then, make them your own. Infuse your writing with who you are. We already have a Diane Warren, Ja Rule, Mark D. Sanders, Bruce Springsteen, and Jason Blume. Dig deep and let the world see inside the only person on this Earth that is you. Then your writing will be as distinctive and exceptional as you are.

THINKING IN A STRAIGHT LINE

I learned a lot about songwriting when I had an opportunity to teach it as a participant on a panel at the Septien Vocal Studios in Dallas. The other teachers on the panel included music publishers, record label execs, and Robbie Nevil. Robbie is best known for "C'est La Vie," the hit that he sang and wrote in the '80s, but as a writer/producer he's gone on to great success with artists including Destiny's Child, Jessica Simpson, Babyface, and K-Ci & JoJo. I'd never met Robbie before the weekend of this workshop but I felt a strong connection, and I had a feeling we'd be friends.

So there we sat facing more than a hundred aspiring artists and songwriters, all hungry for the magic answers that would lead them to success. At one point during the panel discussion Robbie said, "Let's look at a professional songwriter's process. Jason, as I look out at this audience a title hits me, "How Bad Do You Want It?" Show the audience how you would approach writing this song."

My first thought was, "I'm going to kill him for putting me on the spot this way!" My second thought was, "I love that title." In the minutes that followed, years of developing my craft paid off.

My first impression was that this title would be best suited for a female singer, and because of the suggestive nature of the words the style of music would likely be R&B or R&B/Pop. I thought it would probably work well to have the "It" referred to in "How Bad Do You Want It" be a reference to love—as opposed to the more obvious sexual connotation that it implied. Having it be a love song, as opposed to a purely sexual message, was something I was more comfortable with, but the title lent itself to working either way. By ending the chorus with "How bad do you want *my love*" instead of the expected sexual meaning of the line, I could end the chorus with a lyrical twist that would serve as a payoff to tie it all together.

In thinking about how to approach the lyric, I knew that I'd want my title to appear in my choruses, and I needed my verses to provide a reason for this woman to ask, "How Bad Do You Wannit?" I imagined a sexy woman with "attitude," hands on her hips, looking at some guy and saying, "So, you say you *really* want me? How bad? How bad do you want my love? Bad enough to walk through the fire for me? Bad enough to get down on your knees? Bad enough to give up messing around with other women? Do you want me bad enough to treat me the way that I deserve to be treated?"

I started tapping out a groove with my hands on the table in front of me. Over that beat I sang a melody that repeated short, catchy phrases. I blew the audience and Robbie away. It wasn't that I was brilliant. I used specific skills that almost anyone can learn. Creative individuals aren't exactly known for their logical approach to things. We tend to be more intuitive than logical. But by thinking in a linear fashion, we can craft lyrics that unfold in a straight line and clearly lead the listeners to the title. By using short phrases and the tool of rhythmic repetition we can write melodies that are memorable.

Before leaving the stage I decided to turn the tables and put Robbie on the spot by asking him to write "How Bad Do You Wannit?" with me. A few months passed before schedules allowed us to get together. We had a great time finishing the song and I love it.

Exercise

Take a moment and answer the following questions:

- ✓ How badly do you want it?
- ✓ What price are you willing to pay in terms of an investment of your time and money?
- ✓ Are you willing to keep working on honing your craft in the face of stinging rejection?
- ✓ Do you want it badly enough to accept that the odds are against you—and to do it anyway?

Sometimes those who want it the most and are willing to do whatever it takes—and not necessarily the ones with the most talent—are the ones who achieve success.

TARGET YOUR MARKET

In the early days of my songwriting journey I went through incredible frustration. I wanted success desperately and it seemed impossible to reach. Looking back, I can see that one of the biggest obstacles was my failure to differentiate between songs that were appropriate for myself as a performing songwriter, versus those songs that were appropriate to be pitched to other artists. On some rare occasions they were one in the same. But more often I wrote the kind of songs that an artist like Joni Mitchell or Cat Stevens might write and perform—except mine weren't nearly as good. Then I became angry and indignant when publishers and recording artists weren't interested in my work.

If your goal is to have your songs recorded by artists other than yourself, you need to write the kinds of songs that are currently being recorded by artists who do not write their own material. This might seem obvious, but it's something many developing writers seem to ignore. I did.

It never occurred to me that the songs I was writing were the kinds of songs that artists wrote for themselves. It was like trying to sell ice to Eskimos. I didn't want to change anything about my songs—I just wanted them to be hits on the radio. I'd like to eat pizza and Godiva chocolates every day without gaining weight, but that's not going to happen either. I want to reiterate that there was nothing wrong with writing songs for my own enjoyment, or for myself as an artist. The problem was that I was confusing them with the kinds of songs that I could get other artists to record.

Alanis Morissette can say anything she wants to lyrically because she doesn't have to pitch her songs to publishers, who pitch them to record labels, who in turn pitch them to producers and recording artists. If she likes her song she can record it whether people understand the lyrics or not. Same thing if you're Rufus Wainwright, Country star Clint Black, india.arie, Michelle Branch, Sting, Lauryn Hill, or if you're performing your own material on the Folk circuit.

These artists are *performing songwriters*, meaning they record and perform their own songs. It's not that performing songwriters don't have to write great songs. They do. But their intention is not primarily to get other artists to record their songs. Singer/songwriters are selling a total package that includes their sound, image, and songs that are unique to them. Their songs help define and carve out their artistic identity. The songs they write are not held up to a lower standard, but to a *different* standard than those songs that are crafted with the intention of being pitched to outside artists.

While there are no "rules" for successful songwriting (only "tools"), I've observed that artists who record songs that they do not compose tend to record songs that are more literal lyrically. If you examine the songs on commercial Country radio, as well as the songs recorded by Pop artists who don't write their own songs, you'll notice that the lyrics of these songs are typically easy to understand. They make perfect sense. Think for a moment about the hits that have been recorded by Celine Dion, Whitney Houston, Garth Brooks, Christina Aguilera, Ricky Martin, Martina McBride, Marc Anthony, Faith Hill, or any of the other superstars who don't typically write their own hits. The lyrics to these songs aren't vague, obtuse, or shrouded in symbolism. They tell a clear story in a linear fashion and simply say what they need to say. They maintain continuity by having each line logically lead into the next. Like laying bricks, there are no gaps in information.

Songs that are recorded by *outside* acts tend to fit into one of the most popular song structures and employ rhymes in the expected places. But for songs that are recorded by *self-contained* artists and bands (those who write for themselves), there is more latitude to stray from these tools.

Melodically, the hit songs that are not written by the artist, but by *outside songwriters*, typically contain lots of melodic and rhythmic repetition. This helps them to be catchy, hooky, and easy to sing back. The melodies written by artists who are writing for themselves still need to be strong and memorable. They typically incorporate many of the tools that make melodies easy to sing and remember, but they might be even quirkier and more distinctive since part of their job is to help define the artist's unique identity.

If your goals or talents do not include being a recording artist, and your style of writing does not seem consistent with any artists who are currently successful, you have a few options. You might alter your writing, gearing it more toward those artists who are currently recording material written by outside writers. You might try to find developing artists to collaborate with; you can let them be the voice for your songs. Another option is to accept that the style in which you choose to write is not likely to be commercially successful in the current marketplace—but do it anyway because you enjoy it.

Or you could try what I did for so many years. Write songs that have no outlet in the current market and be angry and frustrated because no one wants to publish or record your songs. This last option is *not* recommended.

Exercise

Select an artist whose work you enjoy and respect, and who typically does not write his or her own songs. Give yourself an assignment to craft a song for this artist that would be perfect to take him or her to the next level creatively.

Analyze those songs that have been successful for this artist. What melodic and lyrical tools and techniques did the writers use to craft successful songs that you love? Write something you love that would be appropriate for this artist to record—and be sure to imbue your song with original, fresh ideas, musically and lyrically. But take care to avoid the temptation to copy what that artist has already done.

ONE SONG CLOSER

**"It takes courage to grow up and turn out
to be who you really are."**

—e.e. cummings

This morning I received one of *those* phone calls from my music publisher in New York. He'd just finished listening to the latest song I submitted; this one was intended for consideration for a particular rock singer's upcoming album. I'd cowritten the song with one of the hottest writers on the charts, and considered it a major coup to be able to work with him.

This song was a departure for me. We'd taken some chances and written a melody and lyric that were harder edged and quirkier than what I typically write. The demo sounded incredible. My cowriter and I felt so sure that this song was a hit that I laid the hype on extra thick when I Fed Ex'd it to my publisher. My cover letter said I "know" this one will be not only a smash single, but also the title of the album.

My publisher hates the song. This is not one of those songs he's on the fence about, or believes is only "pretty good." He said it sounds "forced, fake, and contrived," does not sound like real rock, and doesn't even come close to fitting in with the intended project. Ouch. ("But what do you *really* think?") I somehow managed to sound unemotional and professional, and to say that although I was disappointed, I appreciated his input, and his willingness to be honest with me.

The publisher's feedback was especially disturbing in light of a conversation we'd had a few weeks earlier. We had discussed his setting up a writing trip to Los Angeles for me and he mentioned the names of a couple of potential collaborators who are enormously successful, long-established writer/artists—household names. These are artists I should have been ecstatic to write with, but I wasn't.

The individuals he wanted me to work with had enjoyed their biggest successes in the 1980s. While their classic songs are still generating huge royalties, they don't have any recent hits, and are not writing what I consider to be cutting-edge music. I felt insulted to be relegated to the "Old Farts Club"; to be lumped with writers who are past their prime. It wasn't just that I felt emotionally wounded and offended; I feared that being seen in this light would eliminate many future opportunities and have disastrous implications for my bank account.

My publisher explained that his suggestions for collaborations had been intended as a compliment—as a demonstration of his faith in me, rather than an insult. He said he felt my greatest strengths as a writer included my ability to craft "classic-sounding" melodies and lyrics, and to write songs that did not merely reflect the latest passing trend. While I was pleased to know that he felt I could write sweet, romantic love ballads, I did not want to be pigeonholed into writing *only* this kind of song. I wanted a shot at writing with some of the writers, artists, and producers who were currently on top of the charts.

I asked my publisher to put the L.A. writing trip on hold until I'd turned in half a dozen new songs that I felt would demonstrate my ability to compete with the younger, hipper writers. I hoped that when he heard these latest songs, he would revise his impression of me, and hook me up to collaborate with some of those hot new writers and artists who were writing current hits.

The song he hated was the first song in that new batch intended to convince him that I am a true chameleon, able to write in the latest style. Apparently it didn't work. In fact, it had the opposite effect. He urged me to stop fighting what comes naturally. I was reminded that even my recent successes with Britney, the Backstreet Boys, and LMNT were songs that could be categorized as classic-sounding love ballads.

Ironically, just a few weeks prior to my writing this "fake, contrived" song, my publisher had urged me to "push the envelope." He said that the only way to get cuts was to take chances creatively. He suggested that I look for provocative, attention-grabbing titles, fresh, emotion-provoking lyrics, and melodies and grooves that were unique and unpredictable. He said that nine out of ten times this sort of creative exploration would probably not result in a successful song, but that sometimes that tenth song would be the ticket to something very special.

I pushed the boundaries, and this time it didn't work. Should this song be written off as a failure because it didn't get recorded? Should I conclude that I can't write anything but sappy, middle-of-the-road love songs? Have I agreed to be docilely led out to pasture? No way! I've decided to keep pushing the boundaries of my creativity. Not just because I want to be part of the lucrative commercial market, but because my heart's drawn to the challenge of exploring new forms of creative expression.

On the other hand, I'm beginning to understand that we all have natural gifts and talents, and I've decided to stop begrudging mine and start honoring them. No matter what the latest musical trend has been, whether it was Rap, Heavy Metal, Techno, Grunge, or Neo-Soul, there has always been room on the radio for a beautiful love song, and I suspect there always will be. In any case, I'm now one song closer to writing one that is truly extraordinary.

I thoroughly enjoyed both the writing and demo processes when I wrote that song my publisher hated. I dug deep into areas of my creativity that I don't often tap into. I felt stimulated and challenged. That song helped me to grow creatively, and someday it might be perfect for a different artist's album.

Exercise

Take a moment to think about who you really are as a writer. Then answer the following questions:

- ✓ What are your strengths?
- ✓ Which aspects of songwriting come easily for you—and which ones are a struggle?
- ✓ Which styles of music are those that flow out of you effortlessly?

Now, begin a new song that incorporates what you do best.

Another time, challenge yourself by writing a song in a style in which you rarely, or never, write.

FINDING ORIGINAL SONGS

I recently had the opportunity to evaluate singers and songwriters at a huge Music Expo. They came to Nashville from every corner of the country for their chance to be heard by music business professionals. Each singer and writer had an opportunity to perform two songs while I and the other evaluators filled out checklists, rating their vocal performance, stage presence, image, and songs in a variety of areas.

Throughout the day I worked hard to smile my most reassuring smile, because most of the performers seemed petrified. The majority of them were good, but not exceptional. But there were two problem areas that I noted over and over again, and they both related to the choice of material.

The singers were showcasing by singing to instrumental tracks (as opposed to with a live band), and many of them chose to use karaoke tracks of well-established hit songs. After sitting through at least a dozen renditions of "Unchained Melody" and "Titanic's" "My Heart Will Go On," I began wishing that I had been on the Titanic.

The singers who chose to perform these songs did themselves a huge disservice. First of all, they were setting themselves up to fail by inviting inevitable comparison to the perfect studio recordings we've come to know by Celine Dion and LeAnn Rimes.

Unless they dramatically altered the interpretation of the songs (which would be very difficult to do since they were singing to sound-alike versions of the original music tracks), it was unlikely that they were going to sound as good as the original recordings. The majority of the singers seemed to be attempting their best impersonations of Celine or LeAnn, copying every vocal lick and nuance. Even if they had sounded as good as the artists who made these songs famous, they were failing to present themselves as artists with original, identifiable sounds.

Equally problematic was the fact that these singers missed the opportunity to use songs to help carve out a unique identity for themselves as artists. Every vocalist doesn't have to be able to write her own hit songs—but she does have to be able to find them. Tina Turner is strongly associated with the song "What's Love Got to Do with It." The words and music, when coupled with her one-of-a-kind interpretation, convey an attitude that is uniquely "Tina Turner," yet she did not write this song.

If you are an aspiring recording artist, an important part of your job is to find those songs that are potential hits, those that will help delineate an identity that is distinctively you. There are a variety of ways that you can find original songs. Many music publishers will send you songs if they believe you have star potential. Likewise, many developing songwriters would be ecstatic to have you use their material for live performances and to present yourself to record labels. In some instances, songwriters may even let you add your voice to their instrumental tracks, saving you the expense and time of fully producing your own demo.

You will need to have a good recording of your voice to play for publishers and songwriters so they'll know which of their songs to pitch you. They'll also need to assess whether they feel strongly enough about your abilities to have you recording their material. Since the whole point is to find strong original songs, and you may not have them yet, in this instance you can use karaoke tracks. But be sure to use songs that express what's special about you as an artist. You might want to use songs that are a bit more obscure, for example, album cuts instead of radio hits that are strongly identified with other artists.

Many cities have local songwriter organizations where artists can network with writers. These organizations exist in every state. The Nashville Songwriters' Association International (NSAI) has more than one hundred chapters—and despite Nashville's association with Country music, NSAI's members write many different styles of music.*

Songwriter events are another place for singers to meet writers. For example, at the annual Taxi Road Rally held each November in L.A., there are typically more than a thousand songwriters in attendance. My guess is that an aspiring artist who distributed a flyer requesting material could find more songs than he or she could listen to in a year.

An excellent way for artists to "audition" original material is by attending performances at local nightclubs. Several Nashville nightspots offer a unique opportunity to hear songs by featuring "Writers in the Round." At these shows, songwriters, including some of the most successful hit-makers in the world, sit in a circle and sing their songs. It can offer those in the audience an opportunity to be among the first to hear these writers' latest creations. Many of these writers would be honored to have up-and-coming artists perform and record their songs.

---

*For an extensive listing of songwriter organizations, see the Appendix of 6 *Steps to Songwriting Success: The Comprehensive Guide to Writing and Marketing Hit Songs*.

When I screened recordings of artists and watched live showcase performances for RCA Records, the assessment I gave most often was, "Good voice—No hits." Great songs that help delineate an artist's unique identity are among the most critical components of that total package that says "Superstar." If you don't write them, find them.

SUCCESS ADDICTION

I've been at Hollywood parties where the typical answer to "How are you?" sounds like a list of the latest additions to one's resume.

For example:

"How've you been?"

"I'm fantastic and life is incredible! I've got cuts with Lonestar, Streisand, and two in that new movie with Mel Gibson."

To a certain extent, most people connect their self-esteem to their financial and career successes. The media and societal influences have trained us to do just that. But those of us pursuing creative endeavors seem to have an exceptionally hard time separating our level of success as artists from our level of self-worth. Our definitions of ourselves become intertwined with how well our work is being received. In a business where success can be fleeting (if it arrives at all), and where so much is out of our hands, defining ourselves according to an arbitrary external measure (i.e., record sales or chart position of our latest single) is a surefire way to get crazy.

Does that mean I don't do it? Ha! I spent more years than I'd care to admit beating myself up for not being a successful songwriter. Then, after achieving what most people would define as incredible success, I beat myself up for not being a *more* successful songwriter. But it wasn't really my ability to write songs that I was attacking. It was the fact that my work wasn't being commercially recognized; I didn't have the hits, respect, or money that I thought would somehow magically transform me.

I remember opening the envelope that held my first big royalty check. It was for a little more than $34,000. This was at a time when I'd been earning approximately $12,000 a year. I walked up and down my hallway on the verge of tears as I kept looking at that check.

Three months later, when an even bigger check arrived, I remember an intensely uncomfortable feeling. I could imagine how a butterfly emerging from its chrysalis might feel. I was being forced to alter my image of myself from a struggling, aspiring songwriter to a successful one. Change is rarely comfortable, even when it's a positive thing, and it took about a year before my new suit seemed to fit properly.

Some things in my life really did change dramatically. For the first time in my life I was able to buy a nice house and a fancy new car. I got out of debt, and instead of worrying about how I would pay my bills, I found myself learning about investments and planning for my financial future. (Prior to my first hit my idea of "financial planning" meant thinking about who I could borrow the rent money from.)

My newfound success as a songwriter opened the doors for me to collaborate with successful writers whose skills I was in awe of. And of course, most importantly, I got to say, "I told you so" to all of those people who'd said I'd never make it. Now that I was considered an "expert" with hits on the charts, I gained the credibility to take my song-writing teaching to the next level. So there's no doubt that many aspects of my life were changed by having hits.

It's an old adage that success is an inside job and it's true. Success is terrific. I love having hit songs, successful books, and money in the bank. I'm deeply grateful for all that I have—but none of it "fixed" me.

I wasn't aware of it at the time, but in retrospect I can see that I imagined success would somehow heal all the old wounds that were inflicted when I felt inadequate as a child. I thought having hit records would take away the scars from every time I'd been called a name or beaten up by a bully. I expected money and recognition to fill holes inside my soul that had nothing to do with whether I could write good songs or not. Success really can do all of those things and more, but only for a very short time. Then the thrill wears off and we need another success. And then another. I had to find other, more lasting ways to make peace with my past.

Success is wonderful; I hope you'll achieve lots of it. But be forewarned—hits and money don't fix everything.

DO WHAT YOU LOVE

The conventional wisdom is that it's easier to get an uptempo song recorded than a ballad, and easier to get a song with a positive message recorded than one that's sad. Why? Because there are typically more slots on most albums for uptempo songs, and those uptempos that have depth, or "meat," are the ones that are most in demand. But in my experience, I've found it's easier to get one exceptionally powerful, emotionally wrenching ballad that came straight from my heart recorded than a dozen really good positive, uptempo songs that are pure craft and no feeling.

In a recent demo session I recorded six new songs. Five of them were positive, uptempo songs. There was one sad ballad that came from a deep, vulnerable part of me. One of the songs was a standout. It was the one that everyone was instantly drawn to. Guess which one?

The most successful songs in my career have been ballads. I had a Top Five Country single with "Change My Mind," a singer's plea for his lover to convince him that their relationship isn't really over. "Back to Your Heart," a sad ballad in which the singer begs his girlfriend to show him a way to get back the love they once shared, was included on the Backstreet Boys' *Millennium* album. It was named *Billboard's* "Album of the Year," nominated for a Grammy, and sold more than twenty-three million copies. Britney Spears recorded two ballads that I cowrote. They weren't sad, but they were definitely not the uptempos that we're told we'll have the best shot with. And Country star Collin Raye has recorded four songs that I wrote with the incredible Karen Taylor-Good—all ballads! (My fifth Collin Raye cut was a midtempo written with Gene LeSage.)

So am I suggesting that everyone write ballads? No. I'm saying that I've had the best success with songs that were born in my heart. These were songs that I wrote because I needed to write them, not because I was consciously trying to get a cut.

It's a crazy paradox: a Catch-22. I want success, yet when I chase it, it always seems to stay one step ahead. It probably wouldn't feel very good to have hits with songs I didn't care about. Apparently, I won't have to worry about that. It seems those who make decisions about which songs get recorded can sniff out the real ones a mile away. I'm not skilled enough to make it on craft alone . . . and I'm grateful for that.

Exercise

The best lyrics sound natural, like something you might say in the course of a normal conversation. As I wrote in *6 Steps to Songwriting Success,* "Think Wal-Mart, not Hallmark." Try describing the following situations by talking into a tape recorder just as if you were discussing them with a friend. This will help you to write lyrics that sound down-to-earth and avoid using overly poetic, abstract descriptions.

For instance, to describe your first kiss, instead of writing:

"My heart pounded like the waves against the shore as her lips of honey melted into mine."

You might tell your tape recorder:

"That first kiss is something I'll never forget. We were in my dad's two-tone, blue Mercury, parked outside her house. It was pouring and Joni Mitchell's "Court and Spark" was playing on the 8-track. I thought my heart was going to explode out of my chest. Lightning lit up the night as I took a deep breath, and somehow found the courage to pull her close to me. Oh my God, it was everything I ever thought it could be. I don't even remember driving home, but when I got there, I ran up the steps, two at a time, and burst in the door. My father said, 'What's the matter with you?' And I said, 'I'm in LOVE.'"

Now it's your turn. Switch on the tape recorder and tell it about:

✓ Your first kiss.

✓ The happiest moment of your life.

✓ The end of a relationship.

✓ A favorite memory.

✓   The home where you grew up.

I'll bet some of these images wind up in your songs. And if you really imagine that you're confiding in a friend I'll bet what you say will sound natural and conversational.

TAKE OFF THE PRESSURE

I'm back teaching at Camp SummerSongs in the Catskill Mountains. I didn't really want to go this year. The camp is in a beautiful, rustic setting with no cell phone reception and nowhere to plug in the modem for my laptop. So it meant a week of trading phone calls and e-mails for fresh mountain air, hammer dulcimers, song circles, and folk songs by the pond. I didn't know if I could stand to be so disconnected from the world. Even worse, if I relaxed I might miss an important career opportunity. So along with my guitar I brought a suitcase overflowing with stress and unfinished lyrics that I couldn't quite force myself to work on at home, where I was too busy doing all the "important" things I allow to get in the way of my writing.

At the top of my pile of things to be completed was a lyric for a song I'd started with Melissa Manchester. Before I go any further I've got to explain that, to me, when I was a teenager Melissa Manchester was the Beatles and Elvis rolled into one. I idolized her writing and her singing. I bought every album and memorized every song. At one point I'd pleaded and cajoled my father into bribing the security guard at a club to let me in even though I was underage.

So you can imagine how sweet it was when Melissa and I became friends and cowriters. It was wonderful to learn that the woman behind the music is just as special as those songs. But she sure is a demanding collaborator. She pushed me harder and was less willing to settle than anyone I could remember writing with. Although I work differently with different collaborators, in this instance I was primarily writing lyrics and Melissa's main contribution was her gorgeous, classic melodies. At one point when we'd finally agreed on a lyric, Melissa changed the melody to make it even stronger, but this meant I had to rewrite my lyric, almost from scratch.

This particular time I was really struggling. I'd revisited the lyric several times and hadn't made much progress. Okay, I'll admit it: I was intimidated. No, I was beyond intimidated, because it was not only a difficult lyric to nail—but this was *Melissa Manchester* I was working with! There were several additional lyrics waiting to be rewritten in that pile. Each had its own reason why it was difficult for me to work on it. They'd been nagging at me, demanding to be finished for anywhere from a couple of weeks to a few months.

My first morning at camp I decided that this enforced relaxation was just what the proverbial doctor ordered. I set off walking to revisit my favorite spots. I decided I deserved a week's vacation from the self-imposed pressure to write a hit. Those lyrics could wait.

The pond was even prettier than I'd remembered. The cattails were tall and the water was alive with frogs and fish. The water lilies seemed too pretty to be real. As I continued along the trail I saw deer tracks and stopped to talk to a goose. I thanked God for this beautiful day and the wonderful life I'd been given.

I found myself meandering off the path and going deeper into the woods. Unconsciously, I started humming one of my songs. It was one of those that were waiting to be rewritten. I had decided not to work, but this wasn't work. It was a joyful, natural extension of who I am. Within the next few hours, drafts of two lyrics had been rewritten—because there was nothing else in the world that I'd have rather done more than create in such a beautiful setting. Since there was no television or Internet access, after a long day of teaching I spent the night in bed with a good novel, and as a bonus found a couple of interesting song ideas hiding in those pages.

The next morning I woke up feeling peaceful. I looked at the notebook I'd left on the dresser and made a couple of minor changes in yesterday's lyrics. I knew they were good. But no more work! This time I hiked the Covered Bridge trail. When I came upon a waterfall the beauty was so intense that I started to cry. I knew I was seeing what heaven must look like. I'd read about people finding their "magic spot"—that place that speaks to their heart and whispers their name. I knew I had found mine. When I tore myself away to head back to teach my morning class I found myself thinking about the lyric for that Melissa Manchester song. I bet you can guess the end of this story. The lyric's finished and I love it.

When I took away the pressure and the demand to produce a hit, I allowed my creativity to do what it does naturally, which is to flow and express itself. We all need to find our magic spots, those places, both physical and emotional, where our creative self can feel safe and free to express itself.

Maybe there's something to this relaxation thing. I'm having a great time *and* I'm accomplishing things I couldn't do at home. I'm a happy camper (literally). I might have to try relaxing more often.

THE TEACHER LEARNS

This past May, when it was time for the option for my staff-writing deal to be exercised, it was a great feeling to know that there was no doubt my contract would be picked up for another year. My confidence came from knowing that there was lots of money in the pipeline, primarily thanks to the more than forty-five million albums sold by the Backstreet Boys and Britney Spears, who had recorded my songs.

Since the payment that would be given to me when the option was exercised is actually an advance against my own future mechanical (sales) royalties, my publisher had nothing to lose by extending my deal for an additional year. Essentially, the company was lending me my own money—with a guarantee that they would soon get it back.

When it was time to have the discussion with my publisher that would confirm my next year as a staff-writer, I thought it was a good time to bring up some of my concerns. I told him that I felt my songs weren't getting the attention they deserved. (Note: No songwriter in recorded history has *ever* felt his or her songs were getting the attention they deserved.)

The company had recently signed a slew of new "high-ticket" writers. These writers could command a substantial advance because of their recent hits, and it seemed to me that their songs were the only ones that the songpluggers were focusing on at pitch meetings. As we were about to enter my new contract period, I felt the time was right to voice my concerns and get some assurance that I was still a valued writer, and that in the coming year getting my songs recorded would be a priority for the company.

I expected to be told that *of course* I was valued, that my songs were being pitched much more than I realized, and that they would certainly continue to be pitched throughout the coming year. I was totally unprepared for the response I received. My publisher looked me in the eye and said that most of my songs were not being pitched because they weren't as good as songs some of the other staff-writers were turning in. I felt like I'd been punched in the stomach.

He elaborated, saying that I had been focusing on writing the kind of Pop songs I'd previously gotten recorded by Britney and the Backstreet Boys, but that the market had changed. These artists were growing up and wanted to go in some very different artistic directions. Instead of recording the straight-ahead Pop songs that I'd had success with, they were looking for more innovative, cutting edge, Urban-sounding tracks. They were working with producer/writers whom they hoped would provide them more artistic credibility than the ballads that I'd had success with.

He continued that while I'd been concentrating on writing Pop songs, I hadn't kept up with the trends in the Country music market. In his opinion, my Country songs and demos were "good," but not competitive with the best songs being written by those new high-ticket writers, several of whom had garnered Grammy nominations since joining the company. He said that I was spreading myself too thin by traveling to promote my book, teaching workshops, and writing greeting cards—while my competition was busy spending one hundred percent of their energy writing songs. Then he played me some of the more innovative songs that the company was having success with.

The following day I spent several hours in meetings with the head of the Nashville office, as well as the entire creative staff. We talked about those songs of mine that had the best shot for success, and we discussed what areas they thought I should work on to get my songs to the next level.

Among the topics discussed were my "predictable" lyrics—those that simply spelled things out, failing to incorporate fresh, new ways of expressing the same old ideas. They suggested that I push the envelope, both lyrically and musically. Then we talked about my demos, which they considered adequate but not exceptional. Finally, they said they'd been giving me enough rope to take care of my business as I saw fit, but that the writers who were having the most success at the company were those who allowed their publishers to take a more active role—booking their collaborations and making suggestions for demo production.

Following these meetings I mentioned to a friend that I knew the meetings had been very productive and positive, but that I felt like shit. I'm the teacher, the one my students look up to. My songs are on albums that sold more than 45 million copies and if that's not enough, I wrote the book on songwriting! I'm the expert. How can my songs possibly be mediocre?

I put on a good act but I was devastated. The worst part was that I knew they were right. It's funny, back in the beginning days of my songwriting I thought everything I did was brilliant. Now that I had considerable success under my belt I knew enough to know where my songs missed the mark—and I knew in my heart that my recent songs weren't exceptional. I couldn't snap out of my funk for several weeks. I had a profound sense of being a fraud. After all, I couldn't master some of the very skills I was teaching.

I made a decision to give songwriting all I had for the coming year and if things didn't go well I would reassess my career goals at that time. I turned my calendar over to my publishers and said, "Fill it up with the best cowriters you can hook me up with." I asked for help with my demo production and received some fantastic recommendations. I started writing songs every day and loving it more than I had in a long time.

The moral? We can always learn more and continue to improve our skills. But in order to do that we have to be willing to take an honest look at our strengths, as well as those areas that still need work. My songs (and their writer) grew stronger as a result of swallowing my ego and acknowledging that in spite of my successes, I still had work to do.

Postscript: My songs have gone to the next level. It felt great to hear my publisher say that the last five I delivered are the strongest songs and demos I've ever turned in. They've earned the attention of my publishers and are getting pitched as much as I could hope for... well, almost!

Exercise

What are those areas you need to work on? Are your lyrics as interesting and fresh as the current radio hits? How about your melodies? Are they instantly memorable? Predictable—or innovative?

- ✓ List those obstacles that stand in the way of your success.
- ✓ Formulate a game plan; make a commitment to overcome each obstacle that stands in your way.

RICH OR POOR, IT'S NICE TO HAVE MONEY

I was miserable for so many years. There were several parts to this misery equation and the sum of the parts equaled frustration, depression, and unhappiness:

- I was spending half of my waking hours doing something I hated.
- I had neither the time nor the energy to do what I *really* wanted to be doing.
- I was struggling to survive financially, and sinking deeper and deeper into debt.

Back when I was working temp jobs, when I put on a jacket and tie to go to work in an office, I would wear a matching persona. I was a great temp and often got offered full-time positions, which I turned down. I could play the part exceptionally well, but I felt like I was smothering the artist inside of me. When I got home from work I was exhausted and depressed—not exactly an emotional state that's conducive to being creative.

I wound up in therapy. My therapist said that my problem was that I was focusing on a future that might, or might not, ever materialize. He said that I needed to be happy today. He made a convincing argument that success comes with its own share of stresses, heartaches, and troubles, and that although my life would certainly be different, I probably wouldn't be any happier if I were successful.

This guy was a professional. It all made sense and I believed him. So now I had an additional problem. I had to accept that in addition to being miserable from being poor and working at low-paying jobs that I detested, now it was my own fault that I wasn't finding happiness in the journey.

I worked hard to stay in the moment and to appreciate my life "as is," but it didn't work very well. No matter how I tried to convince myself otherwise, deep in my heart I knew that I was unhappy. I also knew that my purpose on this Earth was not to be typing, filing, unloading freight, shredding paper, or answering phones.

Even working those temp jobs, it was a constant struggle to keep my head above water financially. I didn't make much money and a big percentage of what I did earn was being used to record demos, buy blank tapes, and pay for postage and envelopes. And that doesn't include the money I was spending on voice lessons, as well as a rehearsal studio when I was working with a band.

Of course, there's the famous story of my eating cat food, but that happened only a few times. The long-term reality was that I lived a hand-to-mouth existence without a savings account or health insurance. I didn't starve, but my food budget only allowed for a diet of mostly eggs, macaroni, generic hotdogs, and whatever was on sale. I have vivid memories of going to the market and weighing my produce twice to be sure that I'd have enough money to pay for it when I got up to the cashier. It took a toll emotionally and physically. Yet, I kept trying to convince myself that I should be happy *now*. I worked hard to believe that hit records, the respect of my peers, and financial security would not hold the keys to my happiness.

Bullshit. It was a big pack of lies. It feels horrible to work at a job we hate. It feels even worse to live day in and day out with just barely enough money to get by, growing credit card debts, and the constant juggling of bills. It was exhausting and demoralizing. Not feeling those feelings would have been denial.

In retrospect, I can say that I'm *immeasurably* happier doing what I love, and being paid well for it, than I was when I was struggling. But it's not just about the money. Don't get me wrong. As my grandmother often said, "Rich or poor—it's nice to have money."

Money's great. It can buy some wonderful things. But even more than my nice house and car, I love the sense of security I get from knowing that I've got a financial cushion. It's wonderful having the time, freedom, and support of a publisher so that I can do what it is that I love—and what feels consistent with who I am. It's fantastic knowing that I don't need to worry about paying an unexpected doctor's bill or getting a car repaired, and I love having the money to travel. These things are great. But they can't compare with the sense of satisfaction and accomplishment I feel, knowing that I've achieved a goal that was so difficult to attain.

Looking back, I wish I could have found ways to enjoy the journey more, instead of being so focused on the destination. I wish I could have been more grateful for what I had, instead of focusing on what I wanted. Unfortunately, that's not the way I was built.

There's great wisdom in the advice to live each day and to enjoy each moment to its fullest. There's also great wisdom in this statement: If you've got to eat a plate of poop, hold your nose and do everything you can to make the best of a lousy situation. But don't compound the problem by telling yourself that you should enjoy it as much as Häagen-Dazs.

FORGET ABOUT IT

There's an allegory about a centipede. The way the story goes, someone asks the centipede how it knows which of its hundred feet to move next. When it starts thinking about it, the poor thing gets so overwhelmed that it can't move at all. I've seen a similar thing happen to songwriters I've coached; I've also experienced it myself.

I've noticed that many developing writers seem to go through an especially frustrating phase after they've learned all the basics and are beginning to get close to the next level. As the success they want so badly begins to come into view, they start to second-guess themselves, censoring and criticizing everything they write, until the resulting songs are nothing more than self-conscious, perfectly crafted exercises, devoid of heart and genuine emotion.

It's true that the competition vying for a slot on a major artist's album is fierce. There's no doubt that we need to write exceptional, original, unique songs in order to have a shot at edging out our competitors. For those writers who earn their livings writing songs, the pressure to write consistently at that level is intense. If they don't continue to write songs that generate royalties, they'll be looking for new careers. For those who are trying to break through, the drive to write that first hit can be just as strong, if not stronger.

So the natural inclination is to try harder, to push ourselves further, in an attempt to control the outcome. In some ways, that's a good thing. It can inspire us not to settle for less than our very best work. But when our creativity becomes motivated by the desire for commercial success, or the fear of *not* achieving it, the result can be the opposite of what we want. When this occurs, some writers become immobilized. Others stop trusting their gut instinct and try to "chase" the radio, meaning they emulate songs that have already been hits instead of creating something new and special—that is, the next trend. It's easy to forget that the songs that play on the radio today were written at least a year ago, and, in some instances, many years before that. If you write what's currently hot on the radio, you've already fallen behind.

It's not easy to ignore or forget that we want to be successful. But when we're in the midst of the creative process, we need to block out all considerations except bringing forth the song that's waiting to emerge. Be kind to yourself and respect your creativity. Later on you can invite your internal critic to do its job and you can rewrite. Tomorrow you can obsess about whether a publisher will like your song and who might record it. But when you sit down to write, leave all of that stuff outside your creative space.

Learn the tools of effective songwriting. Allow them to seep into your consciousness and become a natural way for you to express yourself. Then forget about them and write what you feel.

MUSIC AND ART

The first time I ever attended a songwriting workshop I knew that my ultimate goal was to be successful enough as a songwriter to gain the credibility to teach someday. In fact, when I learned that the Backstreet Boys had recorded my song, "Back To Your Heart," my very first thought had nothing to do with how much money I would earn. Although I admit that thoughts of my bank account weren't too far behind, my initial excitement was knowing that having a song on one of the biggest-selling albums of all time would guarantee me a level of credibility as a songwriting teacher that no one could ever take away.

I probably feel more centered and more alive when I'm teaching songwriting than at any other time. At yesterday's Washington, D.C. area workshop, I gave a six-hour presentation. When it was over I was physically and mentally drained, but at the same time exhilarated. I felt as if only ten or fifteen minutes had gone by.

My flight back to Nashville wasn't scheduled until 5:20 p.m. the following day. I could arrange for a late checkout from my hotel and have a relaxing day in bed watching TV or catching up on my rest and reading. But here I was in one of the world's most exciting and culturally rich cities. I got an idea.

I woke up early the morning after the workshop and took a taxi to the airport. I checked my bags, rented a car, and headed straight for the White House. I hadn't been to D.C. since I was a teenager, and I was thrilled to stand in front of the home where so many of our presidents had lived, the place where so much history had unfolded. Then I took the two-mile walk from the Washington Monument to the Lincoln Memorial. Along the way I was especially moved by the haunting sculpture of the Korean War Memorial.

I still had two hours left before my flight, so I headed for the Smithsonian Institute's National Gallery of Art. Even before seeing any of the works of art that are housed there, I was awestruck by the beauty of the building itself. I looked at paintings by the masters—Picasso, Rembrandt, Dali, Van Gogh, Degas, Titian—and even a special display of paintings by Leonardo da Vinci. I was already having a wonderful day when I wandered into the gallery featuring the Impressionist paintings. It was about to get even better.

The first painting that I saw in the Impressionist Gallery was by one of my favorite artists, Georges Seurat. Ever since seeing Stephen Sondheim's Pulitzer Prize-winning Broadway musical "Sunday in the Park with George," Seurat has had a very special place in my heart. The show explores issues I relate to deeply—the price artists pay when they exchange a normal life for one that's dominated by the pursuit of their art; dealing with critics; funding our art; and the scary choice to venture into those uncharted territories where true originality lives, instead of safely following the trends. Combine these themes with extraordinary music and you can easily understand why this show is my favorite. But I digress. Back to the Impressionist gallery...

As I wandered through the rooms filled with some of the world's greatest works by Monet, Manet, Pisarro, and the others who helped define a new way of painting, I was transfixed by some of the pieces. I looked at them from across the room, and then up so close that I could see the brushstrokes. I was filled with feelings I couldn't define. I felt as though I could cry, but I wasn't sad. I was simply overflowing with emotion. I had forgotten that great art could evoke feelings of such intensity in me. I'd felt like this once before—when I visited the Metropolitan Museum of Art in New York City.

I don't understand why those paintings brought up such powerful feelings, because I'm not very knowledgeable about art, rarely go to museums or galleries, and am certainly no connoisseur. There was no logical reason why these paintings should touch something so deep within me, but their sheer beauty circumvented my consciousness to reach my soul—and it felt wonderful.

This reminds me that many years ago I had a friend with a bizarre quirk. He was a huge fan of the singer Barbara Cook, who had made her mark on Broadway and, years later, on the concert stage. Every time my friend heard her sing a certain song, this macho, ex-military man would be reduced to blubbering tears. A mutual friend had forewarned me; still, I could hardly believe it when I sat next to him at a concert. Cook's performance of that particular song had amazing power over him.

Music and art can have that kind of power. Songs can give us strength ("The Greatest Love of All"), solidarity of purpose ("God Bless the U.S.A."). They can help us to express grief ("Swing Low Sweet Chariot") or joy ("Joy to the World"). They help us feel that we're not alone by showing us that the singer and other listeners have felt emotions similar to ours.

It's not easy to express real emotions. Do it anyway. Dig deep within yourself to access those feelings—and your listeners will feel them, too. Have the courage to write songs that are so beautiful they make people cry.